Paris

UNDER THE
OCCUPATION

Paris

UNDER THE
OCCUPATION

ANDRÉ DEUTSCH

First published in Great Britain in 1989
by André Deutsch Limited
105-106 Great Russell Street London WC1

Original French version © 1987 Editions Belfond, Paris
English translation © 1989 The Vendome Press
First published in the United States of America
by The Vendome Press

British Library Cataloguing in Publication Data
Perrault, Gilles
  Paris under the occupation.
  1. France. Paris. Social life, 1939-1945
  1. Title II. Azema, Jean-Pierre III. Paris Sous l'Occupation. *English*
  944.360816
  ISBN 0 233 98511 5

Printed and bound in Italy

CONTENTS

On June 11, 1940, Paris went into premature mourning. People woke to find the streets in darkness, the light obscured by dense clouds of soot. It would take months for the trees to shed their black shroud, and the birds, which had taken flight, were not to return until the autumn. This ominous cloud weighed on us, deepening our anxiety. We had no news at all from the front; we no longer knew whether there still was a front. The government had made its pilgrimage to Notre-Dame, prayed for a miracle, and now twiddled its thumbs on the banks of the Loire. Day and night, sullen columns of refugees passed through the city. First came the convoys of motor cars; afterwards the heavy peasant carts piled high with their depressing bric-a-brac, a mattress on top, where grandmother rode in state like a decrepit idol. Ox carts slowed progress, as did the livestock which some could not bring themselves to abandon. Mothers, haggard and drawn, pushed baby carriages. Refuse carts, fire engines, and hearses were a common sight. Nuns filed past and occasionally the inmates of some lunatic asylum. Above them the sun shone. The town smelled of soot, sweat, and animal droppings. The flow seemed inexhaustible. Like grains of sand in an hourglass, the people of France were pouring from the North to the South.

At midday we were told that German planes had bombed gasoline storage tanks on the outskirts of the city. The following day the wireless announced that Paris had been declared an open city. But before parting her legs of stone for the enemy, one final surge of people flooded out. Panic blocked the exits. Pedestrians traveled as fast as those in cars: it took 15 hours to reach Étampes, less than 13 miles away.

Deserters from the defeated army hurried along the roads, unarmed and unashamed.

The first German negotiator was killed inadvertently in Saint-Denis on the night of June 13–14. General von Küchler wanted to retaliate with a bombing raid on Paris, but was dissuaded by his chief of staff, a man called Marx. The second negotiator waited in Sarcelles for his French opposite number with mounting impatience. The latter, meanwhile, had been unaware that German time was an hour ahead of time west of the Rhine. For the French command, the simple delivery of their capital presented a thorny problem. But there would be plenty of time to adjust their watches to German hours. The only real question was the maintenance of law and order. The enemy imposed a 48-hour curfew, which reflected a certain anxiety, while simultaneously demanding that public services function normally. The French officer pointed out that the second demand rather ruled out the first, unless they were to distribute tens of thousands of passes to essential public-sector workers. All departed to ponder the matter.

An hour earlier, the first German motorcyclist had crossed the Place Voltaire with all the charm of youthful insouciance. The joy of being twenty, and German, in June 1940.

The victorious German Army did not flow into the city like a deep river, but punched its way in like an armored fist, stabbing at the way forward with a fresh finger at each fork in the road. Everything was motorized, with the more cumbersome horse-drawn vehicles left to arrive later in the day. The men were hunched down into their overcoats or leather greatcoats because by now the long-awaited rain was falling on Paris, too late to inconvenience the Stukas though. In that first hour the expressions on the bronzed faces of the victors evinced more lassitude than joy. They had been fighting

and advancing without letup for a month. But, with their mask-like faces and immobile bodies, they appeared welded to their vehicles, increasing our impression of being in the presence of a perfectly efficient fighting machine of steel and sinew. While disbanded French regiments fleeing through Paris did not completely rule out the possibility that the miracle might yet happen, that defeat might not be inevitable, this rigorous demonstration by the Wehrmacht made their own victory a certainty.

· The most famous brothel in Paris, Le Chabanais, was closed along with most other businesses, but a note on the door promised: "The establishment will reopen at three o'clock."

General Dentz, who had just accepted the job of military governor of Paris, with instructions not to defend it, watched from his office window in Les Invalides as the *feldgrau* (field-gray) columns marched over the Pont Alexandre III, across the esplanade, and surrounded his quarters in perfect formation. Quick-spoken officers showed their troops where they would be stationed as though they were on quite familiar territory.

Dentz, expecting the worst, was a little surprised to hear the aide de camp of the new Commandant of Paris, General von Stutnitz, asking for the return of the flags captured by France in 1918. This was the first action taken by the victors. It was almost as if they had fought a war for this, and would be returning directly to Berlin with the standards under their arms. Dentz assured them that he had no idea where they were, and suggested to his visitors that they look for them themselves, since the premises were at their disposal.

Next morning at dawn, however, a vociferous Gestapo officer hauled Prefect of Police Langeron out of bed. Furious at having been made to wait, he reminded Langeron that France had been conquered, asked him if he thought he was still under the orders of "Mandel the Jew," nominal Minister of the Interior, and demanded that he hand over all files from the Prefecture. Roger Langeron, a republican civil servant, took great pleasure in telling him that he was no longer in possession of the said files. He had arranged for their removal at the height of the exodus five days before. Doubting the security of the roads, he had seen to it that the tons of personal files, confidential reports, and political dossiers, which would have greatly facilitated Nazi repression, were loaded onto two barges moored at the Quai des Orfèvres. The barges were now sailing southwards with a team of police officers on board, armed with 55 pounds of dynamite and written orders to scuttle them rather than let their cargos be seized.

Two different episodes with two distinct styles. On one side policemen-executioners; on the other, traditional career officers, victors in 1890, defeated in 1918, confident this time of having won the game, although not to say that they might not have their flags snatched back if the fight started again. Gestapo and Wehrmacht: for four whole years a certain Paris would affect not to know that they were both in the service of Hitler's power.

THE FIRST ENCOUNTERS

The roads, empty at first, became marginally more populous when it was clear that the victorious army would not be shooting at every street corner, and would be sparing the right hands of little boys.

There must be a hundred testimonies concerning the first encounters between Parisians and the Occupier. They tell us precise and contradictory details about everything. Tears were shed at 9:45 when a huge swastika was raised on the Arc de Triomphe, to the sounding of brass and strident military music; a solitary French soldier opened fire in Antony, killing one German and wounding another before being sprayed with machine-gun fire; a hundred onlookers in the Place du Châtelet at 10:20 heard a German officer explaining that France was badly governed; some café proprietors served free drinks to German soldiers; there were some men who offered their services as guides; women who smiled in the expectation of better things. But many shutters remained firmly closed.

In the afternoon, news reached us of the death by suicide of Thierry de Martel, surgeon and chief medical officer at the American Hospital in Neuilly, a well-known Parisian figure. He was the son of the famous society novelist Gyp, herself the great-niece of Mirabeau. Martel killed himself with an injection of strychnine, leaving a note for his assistant to the effect that there would be no point in trying to resuscitate him. This was a typical gesture of a proverbially meticulous man. That same day, fifteen Parisians chose suicide rather than see their city crushed under the enemy boot.

Then German vehicles scattered leaflets informing people that Italy's entry into the war signaled the death of French hopes. For some this four-day-old declaration of war was further cause for despair, but for others it was a comfort: at least there were people more despicable than ourselves.

Two German reconnaissance planes caused a stir by landing on the Place de la Concorde. The Hôtel Crillon and the Ministère de la Marine were hung with swastika banners. At the foot of the obelisk, cameras rolled constantly, filming troops marching past.

After despondency, easily the most widespread feeling was a sickening surprise at the discovery of such absolute betrayal. Although the entry of the German Army into Paris constituted sufficient proof of the superiority of their arms, the gaping crowds would always remember the broadness of their shoulders, the generously cut, flattering uniforms, the incredibly impressive equipment. For many months, the French press had been making sarcastic remarks about German bluff, their plywood tanks, their starving soldiers devouring the famous "eggless omelettes," their young people who our medical authorities assured us had been subjected to such inhuman training procedures that they would crack under the least pressure. Incredulous, housewives now fingered the *feldgrau* jackets, and in working-class districts, mechanics cast connoisseurs' eyes over the hardware. Faced with this unexpected demonstration of physical force and mechanical perfection, Parisians cried out against their French government and the rubbish they had been fed as propaganda. Soon Pétain hit the bull's-eye by denouncing "the lies which have caused us such grave hurt."

At the Arc de Triomphe, where German officers and soldiers continued filing past, Gaudin, keeper of the flame, wounded veteran of the 1914–18 war, whose river of tears had at last run dry, wondered how he should behave when the time for the traditional ceremony drew near. More extreme elements had called on the government to take the remains of the unknown soldier with them in retreat. Gaudin had been notified the previous evening to let the flame go out. One of his comrades, Édouard Ferrand, advised him to wait until 18:25 before taking a decision. But no official was there. A German general was praying, kneeling before the tomb. At 18:30, the two old comrades rekindled the flame themselves before a circle of enemy soldiers standing at attention.

By the end of the afternoon, the Occupiers were out taking photographs of the sights of Paris. Le Chabanais quickly filled with German-speaking clients. Parisians reappeared in the streets, which at dawn—who remembered this now?—had been crawling with German cars equipped with loudspeakers telling the population that they were to be confined indoors for 48 hours. The middle-class areas, emptied during the exodus, remained almost deserted. Even the working-class 14th arrondissement could muster only 49,000 of its 178,000 inhabitants of a few days earlier. Paris had lost between three-quarters and four-fifths of its population.

Since nothing had so far impeded the occupation of the capital, General von Stutnitz decided to stick to a simple curfew at 21:00 hours.

And that was the first of 1,533 nights of the Occupation.

The following day, June 15, the Pigalle cinema opened its doors and numerous cafés put the chairs out on their terraces. The police received orders to direct traffic using the automaton-like gestures of their German counterparts. Most of them took to saluting German officers. Food shops raised their metal shutters. Clocks and watches were set to German time. Licensed brothel-keepers did their utmost to have their establishments classed among those for officers' use only.

Gustave Hervé and Bunau-Varilla took all the prizes in the race to prostitute the press. Hervé, onetime frenzied antimilitarist, then, after 1914, one of that massacre's grimmest apologists, brought out *La Victoire* on June 17. In it he praised Hitler and advised Parisians to welcome his soldiers. The paper lasted three days. Bunau-Varilla's paper, *Le Matin*, gained 523,000 readers in a fortnight.

On June 17, Paris heard Pétain declare on the radio: "I tell you today that you must cease fighting."

On June 18, the military commandant organized a triumphal march down the Champs-Élysées and the Avenue Foch. The enthusiastic crowds consisted largely of German civil servants who had arrived in Paris en masse. The film made by the propaganda services of the Reich would be shown throughout the world as a record of June 14, the day the Wehrmacht entered the capital, to the welcoming cheers of Parisians. It was to be forty years before a French documentary filmmaker unmasked the fraud.

That same day, an unknown number of Parisians heard the call to Resistance broadcast from London by an unknown general with a memorable name.

On June 22, since the use of cars was forbidden, inventive entrepreneurs launched "taxi-bicycles" on an unsuspecting public. On their flimsy coachwork were the words

Vitesse–Confort–Sécurité, "Speed–Comfort–Safety." Tandems were more expensive, but quicker. Horse-drawn cabs reappeared.

The same day, after intense publicity, the first concert by the Occupation army was given in the Tuileries. On the rostrum, Professor Schmidt, inspector-general of military music.

The armistice had been signed that morning at Rethondes, in the same railway carriage that had been used in 1918 to mark Germany's defeat.

Two restaurants, La Tour d'Argent and La Lorraine, published their menus in German in the newspapers. Some shops, on their own initiative, pinned the following notice on their doors: "No Jews." Sometimes the notice was also written in German.

The Russian journalist Vassili Soukhomline, walking round Paris, spotted a few posters on the walls saying "Death to the Boche."

On Sunday June 23, Hitler arrived in Paris at 6:00 in the morning, in a black Mercedes flanked by two other cars. The sculptor Arno Breker and the architects Giessler and Speer were with him. It was his first and last visit to the French capital, which he knew like the back of his hand from having tirelessly studied maps and photographs. He went straight to the Opéra, his favorite building in the world. His almost delirious enthusiasm stunned his companions. He surprised the doorman-cum-guide by remarking that a room had been recently removed. The doorman firmly refused to accept the 50-mark note which the Führer insisted on trying to slip him. Then the motorcade sped on to the Étoile, the Trocadéro, the Eiffel Tower, and the Invalides, where Hitler contemplated Napoleon's tomb at great length. The tour finished up at the Sacré-Coeur, which he did not like, but from where he enjoyed a superb view over his most beautiful conquest. Der Führer left for Le Bourget airport at 9:00 that same morning, declaring to his entourage with genuine emotion that he had just spent the best hours of his life. He had Albert Speer measure the width of the Champs-Élysées and decided there and then that the projected triumphal avenue in Berlin would be twice as wide.

On the evening of June 29, Goering was celebrating at Maxim's in brilliant company. Gorged on caviar and foie gras, he asked how business was doing in France, and announced the imminent setting up of German economic services.

Joseph Goebbels, propaganda minister, visited Paris on July 23. He found it a sad place. He gave orders for his staff to get the wheels of pleasure, activity, and gaiety turning again, "at any cost," telling them that this was all part of the building of the new Europe.

The following day, July 24, the Théâtre des Ambassadeurs announced that it was under new management (having been stolen from Henry Bernstein, a Jew) and opened with a play by Michel Duran, *Nous ne sommes pas mariés*. The notices promised "three hours of side-splitting laughter." Music halls, nightclubs, and cabarets all followed the trend.

Business was booming thanks to the troops who, surprisingly at first, paid for everything scrupulously in "occupation marks." Fancy goods and novelties were among the most sought-after items, but their new regular customers also bought heavy foodstuffs and clothing, which they sent back home in bundles. The story went around that two agents of the Intelligence Service, disguised as German officers, were arrested on the Champs-Élysées. How did the Gestapo recognize them? They were the only officers not carrying suitcases.

One officer, paying for his goods, complimented the sales assistant on the beauty of Paris, and the old lady answered, without malice: "But that's not the half of it, sir, you should have seen it before you came here."

Paris, emptied by the exodus, was filling up again day by day, as the slow columns of refugees made their way back from south to north.

Paris had never looked more beautiful.

Even the most deeply despairing of hearts swelled at the unimaginable splendor of the city. One of the first things the Occupier did was to dismantle the walls of sandbags protecting the major monuments from bomb damage. Private cars, buses, and taxis, all proscribed, were to remain in their garages for four years. Cleared of the mundane flow of traffic, the great avenues took on new and unexpected perspectives. Stone reigned supreme. Released from the thrall of traffic, the eye could rediscover the façades of buildings. The ear suddenly heard old-fashioned urban sounds like the hammering of a cobbler, the clattering of a press, which the internal combustion engine had all but banished from our century. People heard nightingales sing. The air was as pure as country air. Parks and gardens were fragrant with forgotten perfumes. Having thrown off their sooty widows' weeds, trees came into bud earlier in the spring and kept their russet foliage later in the autumn.

But it was even more breathtaking at night. The curfew, fixed at 23:00 on July 27, was put back to midnight in November, "to reward the peaceable and understanding attitude of the people of Paris." The blue-painted street lamps gave out such a pale light that anyone out walking at night had to carry a flashlight, which also had to be covered with a blue filter. The streets, narrower in the deep shadows, seemed more like the lanes of some medieval town. No light filtered out from houses, and the police on the beat, like the night watch of old, whistled furiously at the rare forgetful folk who had failed to put their blackout up in time. The Ville Lumière cloaked herself in darkness, but the full moon exposed her in all her majesty. Unreal, transformed by a lighting man of genius, Paris was like a deserted yet miraculously preserved city of the ancients. In this dreamlike state she offered the double gift of physical beauty and the absence of man. In the intoxicating silence, footsteps rang out in the streets with proprietorial self-confidence. Never had such pleasure been taken in Paris herself since the city had been open to the enemy.

HARDSHIP

But human misery was not long in stalking the nighttime shadows. German time, two hours in advance of the sun, roused the town in the dead of night. Well before dawn—three o'clock by the sun—furtive shadows gathered in front of food shops to watch for the raising of the iron curtain. At a price, concierges rented their porches or an empty cellar to housewives who were determined to be the first: wrapped in blankets, they awaited the end of the curfew before hurrying to the shop next door. Shivering in the chill of the autumn morning, women stood bleakly, hoping for the return of the shopkeeper from Les Halles.

Bread, sugar, and noodles were rationed on August 2. Then in October, butter, cheese, meat, coffee, charcuterie, and eggs. Then chocolate, fresh fish, dried vegetables, offal, potatoes, wine, milk. The ration card was soon as vital as the identity card. And people were hungry.

People were cold. By a merciless trick of fate, winter came early that year, and was one of the hardest since the beginning of the century. Coal was soon in short supply, while gas pressure dropped to a feeble flicker. The pipes burst with the first frost. Family life went on in one or two rooms only, heated somehow or other. Old folks living alone died in their garrets.

The summer, catastrophic but spectacular, had marked the end of a chapter in French history. Winter taught us that conquered peoples have nothing but the bitter chronicle of their miseries.

On November 11, with a desperate desire to reclaim history, the students did manage to add another date to the long list of historic days that have made Paris. They walked in the hundreds up to the Étoile, one after the other, hands on the shoulders of the one in front to commemorate the old victory. All public assembly was forbidden. Taken by surprise, the Germans fired rifles and machine guns, but into the air or at people's legs. The rest of the world thought there had been a massacre. The American press reported 130 dead. There were a few injuries, a hundred or so arrests, and five prison sentences. But the enemy had opened fire. Clearly such a single-file procession would not weaken the resolve of the Wehrmacht. Parisian students had rivaled the panache of the Saint-Cyriens, braving the machine guns in 1914 wearing their plumes and white gloves, before spitting in their palms and picking up shovels in the trenches. People admired their courage, but they had also heard the Germans' warning.

The Occupier wanted to end the year with a suitable tableau, an *image d'Épinal* colored in by Goebbels. On December 14, Paris learned that Hitler had decided "in his magnanimity" to return to France the body of the Duc de Reichstadt. The ceremony took place the following day, the 100th anniversary of the return of Napoleon's ashes. It was held by torchlight, with all the pomp of a Viennese operetta, and without the least popular support. Paris, hungry and frozen, muttered through gritted teeth: "They take our coal, and send us back ashes." But the ticket number III on the cheese ration card that day entitled people to 40 grams of meat as a special treat.

PARIS AND VICHY

On December 23, a crop of red posters appeared on the walls announcing the execution of the engineer Jacques Bonsergent, the first Parisian to face the firing squad, punished for having jostled a German junior officer in the crowd at the Gare Saint-Lazare. As people said, they were quite "correct" during those early months, volunteering their seats on the Métro to women with young children, but they were not quite so sure about what kind of behavior to expect from others. Should a man so far forget his subservient status and be tardy in stepping aside on the pavement, he could expect to be sent reeling into the gutter with a vicious kick to the backside. They were our lords and masters, to whom we owed constant respect. Bonsergent had to die for suffering a momentary lapse of memory.

We suffered hunger, cold, humiliation.

But never ridicule.

For Paris, although often miserable and even squalid, did at least escape being grotesque; the grotesque was concentrated in Vichy. Rather our Parisian papas booted in the rear by Germans than the hysterical admissions of guilt by the gentlemen of Vichy.

Miserable in the extreme, we were informed by these men that it was the love of pleasure that had corrupted our nation. They revealed to the masses that they had been debilitated by reading too much Gide and Proust. They outlawed performances of Molière's *Tartuffe*, sent women back into the kitchen, forbade the employment of married women, denounced teachers as the corruptors of our children, preached the return to the land, condemned divorce, endlessly repeated that our lack of Christian virtues accounted for the French defeat (but did Hitler's Christian virtues account for his victory?), and who finally decreed a national revolution to be led by squires and priests in a kingdom straight out of comic opera (O, my France, they would paint your tortured face with the grotesque makeup of a clown!) and presided over by a washed-up octogenarian, only lucid for perhaps three hours a day, who, thanks to the fervor whipped up by court poets with lines like "Sent by God, instrument of Providence," "his moustache is of the purest white, colour of virtue," "the mystery of the Incarnation," was rewarded with more enthusiastic popular devotion than perhaps any king of France or emperor of the French people.

The Cardinal of Lyon proclaimed: "Pétain is France, and France today is Pétain," while the local *préfet* went one better and called on schoolchildren to "follow the Maréchal as the Hebrews followed the burning pillar in the desert"—a disconcerting exhortation for those pupils who knew that the Hebrews were effectively the very same Jews that their Vichy sugar granddaddy had wholeheartedly persecuted before having them led away to the gas chambers.

But Paris was never Vichy. It could never be, because in the Pétainist imagination it represented the exact antithesis, a debilitating sort of Capua, a Sodom and Gomorrah prey to vices that could never sully the vanguard of morality and order encamped on the banks of the Allier. The France they dreamed of—repentant, virtuous, moral, God-fearing—had no chance of flourishing in that profligate old city. Perhaps it is in the nature of capital cities. Berlin was the most difficult city for the Nazis to win over, not so much because of its working-class population, but because the Berliners' caustic sense of humor relentlessly ate away at the Hitlerian brown varnish. The Paris streets, cynical and skeptical, were disinclined to repeat, along with the villages from the Unoccupied Zone, such devotions as: "The Maréchal can neither be wrong, nor can he wrong us." Not since the Commune had Paris been in such disharmony with the provinces.

More than anything, Paris kept alive a sense of the enemy, while Vichy pretended that the armistice had suspended the march of time and placed France outside the melée in a kind of historical no-man's land. Vichy was in ecstasy over the Maréchal's changing of the guard, tricolores fluttering in the wind, while we hung our heads as the daily Nazi parade marched down the Champs-Élysées. Vichy poked around in the past to expose our sins and preached a future of atonement: we were living the war in the present tense, and realized, to our surprise, that young Englishmen, whose moral fiber did not appear so very different from our own, were making mincemeat of Hitler's airforce, and causing problems for his navy. All too soon, the air-raid sirens were wailing in Paris again. In the daytime we watched the enemy soldiers with amusement, so highly disciplined, running to the shelters breathing down each others' necks. At night we marveled at the fireworks display of German flak, while their searchlights swept the skies for invisible squadrons (we held our breath when a beam picked out a plane, suddenly so vulnerable, to be swiftly joined by one, two, or three powerful beams, bathing the bomber in a fatal pool of light), and in the morning on the lawns of the Jardin du Luxembourg, I would go shrapnel-gathering for my collection. How could we forget the war in Paris?

A sense of the enemy. The enemy was there, omnipresent, omnipotent, like the spider in its swastika web. They continued to frighten us, but we no longer held them in such terrified respect as in those first weeks. We had seen too many suitcases stuffed with the spoils of war, too many bodies flop onto our prostitutes. The climate in Paris is not favorable to the flowering of the myth of racial superiority. And hostility mounted month by month. Not so much the patriotic hatred of the rebel citizen, but more the peevishness of the frustrated consumer. "They are taking everything we've got." The kingdom of Pétain was not spared its share of pillage, and the big cities—Lyon, Marseille—lived like Paris under the urban curse, at a time when even the most miserable peasant could eat his fill, but Vichy, true to type, made of this hardship an expiation propitious for the salvation of the country. Unlike their subjects, we had the organizers and the beneficiaries of this deprivation right under our noses, these wasp-waisted, monocled officers, tasselled swords thwacking against their thighs, the common soldiers whose boots brought an acrid animal smell to the Métro. At first we automatically called them "the Boche," as we had in 1914; but then they became *les Doryphores* (Colorado beetles) because they ate all our potatoes. And when the old Maréchal came back from Montoire talking of Collaboration, Paris was whispering the German definition of the word: "Give me your watch, and I'll give you the time."

The sense of the enemy. Above and beyond all the contradictory reports and polemics, with the benefit of hindsight, one irrefutable fact wraps up the discussion about the state of the Parisian mind. As early as October 8, 1940, Prefect of Police Langeron was called in about anti-German demonstrations in the cinemas during the newsreel. Langeron explained the difficulty of maintaining control in darkened rooms, even if they were packed with police officers. If they put the lights up even briefly to identify the demonstrators, the whole auditorium would side with them. In the end they had to show all newsreels with the house lights up.

That is how Paris remained for four years, in the midst of war, in the midst of life, occasionally for the best, more often for the worst. Riffraff and rabble roamed the streets, but history, the cynical realist, will doubtless be more indulgent towards real ruffians than towards Vichy puppets. In times of catastrophe, there is perhaps more dignity attached to being bad than to being ridiculous.

I SAY PARIS; BUT WHICH PARIS?

After serving their long sentence, four million Parisians were surprised to learn that for *le Tout-Paris*, those same four years had been a time of incomparable brilliance. That select band were unanimous: never had there been so many parties and gala evenings, never had the social whirl been so exciting. Since September 1940, at Bagatelle, the automobile show had ever so subtly transformed itself into the bicycle show. Paris may have been crushed beneath the German boot, but le Tout-Paris did not surrender.

The tourist industry was booming. The enemy garrisons were an entrepreneur's dream come true: a resident foreign clientele with plenty of money to spend, since the paper value of the occupation mark was fixed at twice its real value. And Hitler had decided to offer all his troops a holiday in Paris, his prize conquest. An organization with offices in the Chambre des Députés was in charge of arrangements. It was called *Jeder einmal in Paris* ("Paris for everyone once"), and organized visits by different sections of the German army on a rotating basis. Contingents of soldiers arrived each week from the North Cape, from the Peloponnese, or the farther reaches of the Ukraine, to guffaw at the girls from the Casino de Paris, with tricolored feathers on their bottoms, doing high kicks and singing *Ça sent si bon la France* ("France smells so good"). (But a mole from the Red Orchestra, the Soviet intelligence service, having infiltrated the *Jeder einmal in Paris*, and knowing the provenance of their visitors, was well equipped to tell the Allies a good deal about the Germans' battle plan.) Music halls, cabarets, and nightclubs were packed every night. And *feldgrau* uniforms were in the majority everywhere.

They were in evidence too in the best salons and at the most distinguished tables. For fashionable Paris, it would have been an affront to one's sense of fair play to snub the officers that the capricious fortunes of war had smiled on. Marie-Laure (de Noailles) and Marie-Louise (Bosquet) continued to hold their salons, eclipsed however by Florence (Gould), whose prodigious personal fortune enabled her to keep an incomparably lavish table. The dinner guests *chez* Bunau-Varilla did not find that the little tricolore and swastika flags dancing merrily between the place settings adversely affected their appetites at all. One saw Sacha Guitry, Cocteau, Serge Lifar, Arletty. In fact it would be quicker to list the people one did not see. And one particular trio of Germans was only too delighted to ensure the liaisons between rival côteries and competing salons.

Lieutenant Heller, from the *Propagandastaffel*, an affectionate little man full of reverence for French culture, put about the comforting notion that the spirit would prevail over force, and sent trainloads of writers and artists to Germany who, on their return, would confide with a servile gratitude that a German hand had left a few marks pocket money on their bedside tables every morning. The sculptor Arno Breker, familiar with Parisian ways since before the war, offered for the delight of patrons, his colossal Aryans reminiscent of athletes doped with estrogens. The writer Lieutenant Ernst

Jünger, the darling of le Tout-Paris, was the most sought-after by hostesses because in addition to talent and elegance he possessed the discreet charm of a genuine opposition to Hitler. Aristocrat of the First World War, he became an aesthete in the Second, his tall, slightly affected figure walking the streets of Paris by night before confiding a few derisory remarks concerning the Führer, nicknamed Knebiolo, to his diary. Between conversations with Jouhandeau and Drieu la Rochelle, he would translate for his masters the last letters of our condemned men, or would treat himself to the pleasure of giving a firing squad the order to shoot, to see how a man dies.

Breker's giants were no consolation for our missing statues. That of Mangin, famous butcher of the Great War, had been destroyed as early as June 29, 1940: it was in the same tradition as the reclaiming of the captured flags. In November 1941, 84 pedestals were deprived of their statues at a stroke: more prosaically it was to do with salvaging the bronze. The sympathetic press thanked the enemy for ridding us of unworthy works of art.

The press prostituted itself; writers wrote; editors published; actors played to packed houses; and filmmakers produced some of the most beautiful films ever made in France.

It was a rude dilemma. For bakers could bake and tailors could stitch without problems of conscience. But what to do when the breadwinner wields a camera, or a pen? Jean Guéhenno ceased publishing and noted in his diary: "The writing species is not one of the greatest of the human race." He drew his teacher's salary throughout. Judge Didier was the only French magistrate to refuse to take the oath of loyalty to Pétain, but he had a personal fortune at his disposal.

But no defense pleading could repeal the orders given by Goebbels on July 23, 1940: Paris was to become its old self again, on the double. Shocked by the city's fall, the eyes of the world were on Paris, and would judge Nazism by the kind of fate held in store for the city. "Activity and gaiety," prescribed the good Dr. Goebbels. *Paris, toujours Paris!* That would show the English that they could spare themselves the blood, sweat, and tears promised by Churchill; that would show the Americans, whose press correspondents were numerous, that no crisis need justify the abandonment of their policy of isolationism. Johnny Hess sang in the autumn: *Ca revient, la vie recommence, et l'espoir commence a renaître.* The months passed, world opinion declined in importance, but Paris had to remain the soldier's watering hole, his reward, the Wehrmacht's brothel. The year 1942 was to reveal exactly why the Occupier still wanted Paris to be at play, and we were to be profoundly disgusted at the unplumbed depths of their contempt for us.

But didn't we have to live, and help each other survive? There was no escape from the sadness except in the imagination; our misery could only be anaesthetized by distractions. There was no question of getting away at weekends. To invite friends for dinner without asking them for food tickets was to sacrifice the family's vital nourishment. So we stayed at home, among ourselves. Some people played interminable card games (stocks rapidly ran out). Reading became prodigiously popular. Muffled in layers of woolens, with our gloves on, we read from nightfall, windows shuttered against a hostile world. Any book printed sold right out, and there were an enormous number published (in 1943, as many in France as in the UK and the USA combined), but still

not enough because paper was in short supply. People borrowed more and more voraciously from the municipal libraries; booksellers on the banks of the Seine looked on while people snapped up all their old junk.

It was the golden age of theater. The most appalling show played to packed houses, if only for the animal warmth of simply being there. Lines were long outside the cinema—dream purveyors—for the same reasons. And it was not all mediocre by any means: *Les Visiteurs du soir, L'Éternel retour, Les Inconnus dans la maison. Le Soulier de satin* was put on at the Comédie Française; Jean Anhouilh's *Antigone* and Montherlant's *La Reine morte* were enormously successful productions. The restrictions imposed by the curfew gave the theater an added charm: members of the audience would find actors still in their greasepaint on the platform waiting for the last Métro and could chat with them between stations.

Incredulous, we had seen England hold fast despite the predictions of the sinister Weygand: "She will have her neck wrung like a chicken." England stood firm, but the circling packs of U-boats kept her daily more imprisoned on her own island. The German steamroller had succeeded in flattening Europe. Swastika flags flew over Prague, Copenhagen, Oslo, Warsaw, Amsterdam, Brussels, Paris. In April 1941 they billowed over Belgrade; in May over Athens. In the Balkans, the balance tipped towards Hitler. The English, crushed in Crete, clung to the pebble of Gibraltar and the aircraft carrier Malta.

To hope at all was becoming an arduous, uphill struggle.

In desperation, people turned to the predictions of Nostradamus, of Saint Godefroy, Saint Odile. The irrational reigned, as it always will when reason vacillates in the face of desperate facts. A new rumor ran riot in Paris each week. Mussolini must have been assassinated ten times over. At least once a month the Pope imposed peace. The British had invented a powder to make water burn. General de Gaulle had been killed in the air raids on London, and the intelligence service had substituted his ashes for those of the Duc de Reichstadt, so he now rested next to Napoleon in Les Invalides.

All this was just so much second-rate nervous excitement, like a phantom pregnancy. And then on June 22, 1941, the city experienced its first great collective fever. Hitler invaded the Soviet Union.

And then suddenly, we knew that he had lost the war. None of the Wehrmacht's special announcements, heralded by trumpet blast, could alter our conviction, and neither did the confirmation on English radio that Russian towns were being captured in their hundreds, and Red soldiers too, whole armies at a time. Was it the chauvinistic certainty that Hitler could not succeed where Napoleon had failed? It seemed to us that his fate was being sealed just as fast as his lightning advance. Any invader of the Russian steppe was condemned to fly from victory to victory until meeting final defeat.

December 7 saw the second bout of collective fever: Pearl Harbor marked the entry of the USA into the war. This time it was in the bag, just like 1917. But the news was disconcerting. The Wehrmacht were right outside Moscow, having cut out the previously obligatory part of the curriculum, the crossing of the River Berezina. In Libya, an unknown general, Erwin Rommel, was giving the elegant English generals the runaround. Japan made up its own version of Hitler's blitzkrieg, and the legendary outposts of the British Empire were collapsing like houses of cards. The Axis powers held Europe in their grip, took bites out of Africa and overwhelmed Asia, while their submarines littered the ocean floor with the wrecks of Allied ships.

We were not even out of the trees yet.

RESISTANCE

The shot fired by Fabien on August 21, 1941, marked the turning point in the history of Occupied Paris. "Resistance" is a proud word, with rock-like connotations. The English call it the "underground," which is considerably more appropriate. For the Resistance was indeed digging tunnels, throwing up the occasional molehill to indicate its whereabouts.

On June 14, 1941, all Resistance had meant was wearing a black ribbon or a black tie to mark the anniversary of the entry of the Wehrmacht into Paris. Or, a month later, wearing red, white, and blue to celebrate Bastille Day (1,667 arrests). Or, in the spring of that year, chalking up Churchillian V signs on every available wall, under threat of dreadful punishment if caught in the act.

But then, on July 21, 1941, we woke to find one gigantic V hung from the Eiffel Tower, and others adorning the Chambre des Députés, hotels and requisitioned buildings: the letter V which had been a criminal offense the night before. Gray Wehrmacht trucks flaunting the same letter cruised the streets. One slogan said it all: "Germany triumphs on all fronts." And it was true. They had taken everything, even our V signs. Well played.

Organized resistance is by nature furtive. People speak in hushed tones, with lowered eyes and ears to the ground. Resistance spreads through a city like an subterranean watercourse that has flowed for centuries unseen beneath its buildings. Indeed it surprised many people to read the furious attacks in the Collaborationist press against something which was, as yet, a mythical phenomenon. But subsequently, on leaving a restaurant, say, the discovery that a tract had been slipped into your coat pocket would attest to its reality. Or perhaps a badly printed broadsheet stuck through the letterbox. The signatures were emphatic: "Battalions of Death," "Vengeance," "Volunteer Army." There were at most a couple dozen brave spirits behind it all. The first newspaper, produced by the Museum of Mankind network, was simply called *Résistance*. Groups formed, some of which became networks, movements, while others went to the wall in a few weeks, leaving the historian with just a handful of names or enigmatic pseudonyms.

Agents from London crisscrossed Paris in search of recruits for their Intelligence Service, but, more often, recruitment took place by personal contact or by chance encounter. My parents, both lawyers, joined the Resistance because they had a country house near Reims and a local gendarme put them in touch with some English airmen who had been shot down and needed to get to Spain. My father accompanied such people many times because the route the Allied squadrons took to reach Germany passed right over the Champagne region. The most difficult "parcels" were the Americans fresh from Texas or Oklahoma; what a performance persuading them not to open their mouths in trains! Then British agents started turning up at the house. This was more serious. There was "Alexander," the perfect gentleman, who showed us photos of his dogs back home, who disappeared one day, and years later I was to learn that he had died without talking, and was given this epitaph by the chief of the Special Operations Executive: "He was a tough man among tough men."

I was eleven years old, perhaps twelve. Two brothers older than I and a younger sister. What amazes me today is the fact that no one told us to be careful, to keep quiet. I was never once told not to mention Alexander and those like him. I suppose it just went without saying. Mysterious visitors came and went, and death with them (to this day I cannot see a black Citroën *traction avant* come around a corner—it was the Gestapo's car—without a pavlovian sinking feeling in the gut), while the main purpose in my life remained the improvement of my math grades. So it was that Paris seemed like one of those great silent forests in which the walker subconsciously detects the buzzing of a hive hidden in the foliage of one of the trees. The Resistance was that hive.

The shot fired by Fabien at officer Moser at Barbès Métro station on August 21, 1941, shattered the silence.

Seven Communists died on the scaffold. Vichy dug up some villains in silk to pass sentence on men whose coffins had already been ordered, and even proposed, in an excess of obscene zeal, to have their heads cut off in a public place. The Nazis, disconcerted by such groveling servility, hissed that they had not asked for so much.

In September, eight German officers were killed. On October 20, Lieutenant-Colonel Holtz, *Feldcommandant* in Nantes, was shot. The following day it was Doctor Reimers, adviser to the military administration in Bordeaux.

Twenty-one Communists were either decapitated or shot in Paris; 48 were shot at Châteaubriant; 50 near Bordeaux. The Collaborationist writer Brasillach declared in *Je Suis Partout*: "What are they waiting for? Why not execute the Communist chiefs already in captivity?"

On November 21, a powerful explosion damaged the German bookshop Rive Gauche on the Place de la Sorbonne. One of its window displays featured Henry de Montherlant. Photos showed him aged two with his nurse, and at ten with his mother.

Gabriel Péri and the lawyer Jacques Grunbaum were executed.

The attacks did not stop, nor would they. The massive execution corteges wrenched a cry of disgust from the dedicated anti-Fascist Jean Guéhenno: "Enough of this murder."

Paris was overwhelmed, aghast at the horror of it all. Armed action found few supporters. From Vichy, Pétain called on the population to denounce what he called the assassins. From London, de Gaulle let it be known that "the Germans, if they don't want to be killed, have only to stay at home," but did issue a formal order to cease the attacks so as not to give the Occupier any opportunity to justify a massacre.

The enemy—so the records show us—was doubtful about how to react. Traditionally, hostages were chosen from among people of standing, to have maximum effect on the rest of the population. General von Stülpnagel believed that the trap set by the Communists consisted of pushing him in that direction in order to dig a bloody trench between the Army of the Occupation and the French, whose docility had hitherto been remarkable. He thought he would foil their plot by executing Communists and not leading citizens. On September 28, a month after that first shot of Fabien's, he ordered the setting up in Paris of a permanent "pool" of 300 to 400 Communist hostages, who could then be "fished out" as and when necessary.

It was an act of supreme idiocy. There is a political logic to hostage-taking, which consists of terrorizing a population by subjecting some of its members to the bloody consequences of attacks that had not been sanctioned by all, with the intention of getting people to denounce those individuals who really merited this rigorous punishment. By dragging only "Judeo-Bolsheviks" in front of the firing squads, the enemy were offering all those who were not Communists—the vast majority—the cold comfort of feeling themselves to be irrelevant. They would be able to say to themselves: "Let them kill each other!" As for intimidating the Communists by shooting hundreds of them at the Fort Mont-Valérian, only a regular army general could possibly have hoped it would work. The vow of solidarity linking members of the Party was too strong to be broken by one, or even by a thousand such salvos. A man who died before the firing squad fell in battle every bit as much as an urban guerrilla. By applying mass-repression tactics only to the Communists, the enemy turned them into their fiercest adversaries. Martyrdom sanctified them as champions of the fight to the death. Even the most hostile and blasé observers—those who followed the dreadful raising of the stakes as though from ringside seats—could not but feel a secret admiration for their stoicism. And for those who wanted most ardently to join the Resistance, becoming a Communist was the natural course to take because each German reprisal was further evidence of the high price on their heads.

But their contempt finally outdid their stupidity. The enemy, wanting to avoid a fatal rupture, did however want to ensure that any punishment inflicted on the general population would arouse their hostility against those who had caused it. This discovery stung us like horsewhip. They imposed a 21:00 hours curfew for four days—not unfairly—but also temporarily closed down all "pleasure houses." Sometimes this degrading ritual applied to the whole of Paris, at other times just to the neighborhood where the attack had taken place. I can remember the way people looked, those who were previously indifferent, and even those who despised what the terrorists were doing. They paled with anger at the insult; hatred rendered them suddenly beautiful. Did the Germans really hold us in such contempt as to think that closing restaurants and nightclubs would turn us into traitors overnight? Some of us got a dozen bullets in the heart; other—the rest of us—were to have our stomachs and genitals punished. The enemy was confusing the real Paris with the scum, the dregs, that they encountered nightly in the "pleasure houses."

Notices of execution were posted, bleeding, on the walls.

I used to walk past the occupied Lycée Montaigne four times a day on my way to and from school. Because the pavement on that side was out of bounds, I walked on the opposite side, along the edge of the Jardin du Luxembourg. There was a narrow gate leading into the garden just opposite the school. In the afternoons, draped about on the park benches, available, chattering and giggling, twenty or more French girls used to wait for their German lovers, who would sometimes call over to them from the school windows. The execution notices were put up on the stone pillar just near the gate. We would go through the list of names at school; it did not matter to us whether the dead were Jews or Bretons, Communists or Royalists; they were all equal before the firing squad. And they were men who had said "no!" Youth will always side with such people, which is why Vichy and the Collaborators will never have their names cleared in law, although they periodically seek to do just that.

FAMINE AND GREED

Most Parisians had no direct access to the tragedy, as though it were somehow above their means, but they were able to say at the end of the era, "I lived through it," and it was no mean feat. During those years there was something heroic about ordinary everyday life. The dry statistics speak eloquently. In 1942, the official rations amounted to 1,200 calories a day, when at least 2,400 are considered the necessary minimum. In January of the same year, the mortality rate among the population of Paris was 46 percent higher than the average for the years 1932–38 (it decreased, by contrast, in rural areas). In 1944, a survey of adolescents of fourteen years of age, conducted in the poor districts of Paris, found boys to be almost three inches shorter, and girls more than four inches shorter than average. I was to find out much later, in a learned medical publication, that my own puny arms were an example of a disgrace widespread among people of my generation, on account of nutritional deficiency. There were also weaknesses in eyesight. And tuberculosis killed twice as many young and old people as before the war. In four years, Parisians lost between nine and eighteen pounds each. It was a heavy penance.

Between abstract statistics and the shame and horror of the particular, like the Parisian who strangled his granddaughter because she ate his meat ration, food was the single overriding obsession of those four years. Food haunted the imagination from morning till night. And then at night we dreamed about it. It devoured two-thirds of a poor family's budget.

The shopkeeper reigned supreme. Butcher, baker, charcutier, _crémier_: a new aristocracy was rising. The clientele paid homage to the lady of the house, ennobled behind her cash register, while her scissors, like those of the fates, cut up our food tickets which fell into the special box like so many little snippets of life.

We had to pay court to the grocer because our family network in the country let us down most cruelly. How many long-lost relatives did the war resurrect? All of a sudden the neglected country cousin became the object of great solicitude. The good health of the aunt in Brittany, and that of her three cows, became of vital interest. Family food parcels from the country made all the difference between simple scarcity and true famine, not to mention the possibility of restorative holidays down on the farm with those delectable dunghill smells.

But alas! My mother's side of the family had so few branches, and had suffered so many deaths that there were no roots left. My father's side had imprudently abandoned La Tronquière (Lot Département) two generations back, without leaving a single old retainer.

A pair of scales ruled over the table so that bread might be weighed out to the precise gram, under the watchful eye of families ready to tear each other apart like survivors from the wreck of the ship *Méduse*. Nearly everyone was in the grip of chronic malnutrition; the poor died of hunger. Progressive weakness opened the door to illness and epidemics. The elderly and infirm were decimated. An iron law decreed starvation for those who did not earn enough to purchase on the black market enough calories to ensure basic survival. But if a lawyer could adjust his fees in line with galloping inflation, salaries remained the same, and hundreds of thousands of Parisians did not even earn the minimum necessary to buy the official rations. A survey in 1943, of a sample of 2,729 wage-earning families, found that there was an average of 876 francs a month per family member—or the price of two kilos of butter on the black market.

Some had recourse to the "D" system ("D" for *débrouillardise*, or making do). The city's parks turned into kitchen gardens, and balconies groaned under the weight of edible produce. Tomatoes ripened on south-facing roofs. Potatoes were planted in backyards. In the Jardin du Luxembourg I saw very dignified but desperate old men feed a few crumbs to pigeons, then net them for the pot. People raised rabbits, then faced terrible scenes at slaughter time because the children would be so attached to them. For people in very small flats, a company even suggested raising guinea pigs, "the flat-dweller's rabbit." Cats disappeared. On October 31, 1941, the papers printed an official warning: "Cat-eaters beware!" The text explained that, since they eat rats, cats could be carriers of dangerous diseases. But cats continued to disappear. Hunger is the strongest drive.

Community restaurants opened for the most impoverished. Two hundred thousand Parisians a day ate a meager meal for a modest sum in such soup kitchens. Under the auspices of the church, aid-agencies multiplied. Schoolchildren received protein-supplement biscuits and a little pink vitamin pill.

Such small measures to combat such deep misery! Hunger prevailed. It turned faces ugly, dulled the gaze. It saddened. It humiliated, because when the stomach dictates, the result is degrading. It enfeebled the body and weakened the spirit. Parents were desperate, felt themselves failing as they were powerless to fulfill their basic duty to nourish their offspring. The elderly discovered they were superfluous. People living alone knew they had recourse to no one. Woe betide the poor, the weak, and the alone!

The insolence of the powerful—that is to say the rich—only increased the misery of those already miserable. Ernst Jünger, habitué of the best tables in Paris, had a predilection for the Tour d'Argent, the famous restaurant perching on the top floor of a tall block opposite Notre-Dame. He wrote in his diary on July 4, 1942, after eating there in company with some members of le Tout-Paris—the old and the new: "One has the impression that the people dining up there, eating sole and the famous duck, are looking down, with devilish satisfaction, like gargoyles, at the grey ocean of roofs which conceal the starving. In times like these eating well and plentifully gives a feeling of power."

The cynicism of the full stomach, protected by German bayonets from the riots it should have provoked, knew no bounds. Milk and bread were strictly rationed, but caviar, foie gras, oysters, and luxury game were freely available, for fabulous sums of money. The supply of wine was controlled, but champagne, at prohibitive prices, flowed freely at favored tables and in the nightclubs. The masses could not eat in restaurants without food tickets, but fifty or so restaurateurs obtained a license to offer menus without tickets, reserved for the very wealthy. The black market was king. At the Chantaco, rue de la Pompe, there was no bill; instead, diners received a *millefeuille*— on the house—which signified discreetly that the bill would be a thousand francs per person. (A Parisian worker earned on average twelve hundred francs a month.) And the restaurants in the best locations were not always the most sought after. Initiates spread the word about some coal merchant whose back parlor served ten of the élite for dinner every night, or a boot-mender's workshop which, after shutting up shop for the night, served special guests with foie gras and roast meat washed down with fine wines.

The enemy had fixed the rules of the game.

"They are taking everything we have." We did not know just how right we were in repeating that phrase. Since the armistice, the victors had provided themselves with the ways and means to conduct four years of uninterrupted economic plunder of France. It is traditional for a conquered country to maintain the army of occupation. In 1940, the payment was fixed at 400 million francs a day. It was completely outrageous. French experts worked out that a similar boon sum would actually maintain eighteen million. And barracks costs were not included. Which were sumptuous. Requisitioning of produce and raw materials was at the discretion of the victor, who abused it royally. And then, to crown it all, this masterpiece of brigandage, all soldiers and civil servants working in France, as well as those temporarily resident with *Jeder einmal in Paris*, received in overvalued marks sums representing, in the opinion of the director of the Reichskreditkasse de Paris, 60 thousand million francs a year (when the French budget had not exceeded 54 thousand million in 1938).

Living it up at Maxim's a fortnight after the Wehrmacht arrived in Paris, Reichs-marschall Goering had above all talked business. He had marked out his sphere of interest. While appropriating works of art for his own private collection, the fat Marshal masterminded four years of the systematic pillage of France.

Like leeches, German "purchasing officers" clung all over Paris. Some for the Wehr-macht, the Luftwaffe, the Kriegsmarine, the Abwehr, the SS, not to mention various other organizations invented by Berlin for the occasion. With the fabulous sums provided by the daily war allowance, they harvested the country's vital resources. The bosses were spies and adventurers, their staff common rogues. The most powerful among them was Hermann Brandl, alias Otto, German intelligence agent, whose outfit occupied three blocks near the Avenue Foch. Frédéric Martin, alias Rudi von Merode, drug trafficker and German spy, had his offices on the Rue Pétrarque prior to moving to more sumptuous accommodation in Neuilly. The Belgian Delfanne, alias Masuy, also onetime German spy, gave himself a building on the Avenue Henri-Martin. Henri Chamberlin, alias Lafont, young veteran of juvenile correction institutions, lived at 93 Rue Lauriston. Mendel Szkolnikoff, Jewish adventurer, the most gifted of the lot, became the official purchasing officer for the SS. Well set up on the Rue de Presbourg, he had ten domestic servants, and kept open house at lunch and dinner for twenty-five guests (one day, it is said, Himmler himself) and in four years amassed a fortune of a hundred thousand million of our weighty francs.

They bought anything and everything. By the truckload, by the wagonful. Chamois leather and Old Masters. Turkeys and cement. Lead, nickel, and copper. Cognac fifty thousand bottles at a time, foie gras in tons, meat by the herd, and grain by the boatload. Whatever was for sale, whatever the price, they bought it.

Goering kept urging them on for the kill. August 6, 1942: "You must turn yourselves into hunting dogs, be on the trail of anything which might be useful to the German people...I cannot say too often that I consider occupied France to be a conquered country, and I, for my part, dream of plunder, and frankly...the franc need be worth no more than a certain sort of paper reserved for one particular use....And as for the collaboration of the good French, I look at it like this: they should be giving until they can give no more; if they do it voluntarily I shall say I collaborate, but if they devour it all themselves, then they are not collaborating."

In ever-increasing circles around each purchasing office was an entire bestiary of informers, intermediaries, and businessmen with criminal records. But there were also members of le Tout-Paris, invaluable in establishing the right contacts among the cream of the business community, and sharp lawyers, and ladies who had stepped from the streets to the swanky mansion in three months, and industrialists tempted by the prospect of selling their goods at a hundred times their real value. Real scum and what passed for the cream rubbed shoulders without a second thought in vast apartments piled high with bundles of silk stockings and crates of caviar. The boss of the biggest textile manufacturers in France made deals with a convicted pimp. A commander of the Légion d'Honneur did business with a spy saved from the firing squad by the French defeat. Trafficking with the enemy offers the dual advantage of huge rewards and total impunity.

The results of black-market trading were murderous for ordinary people. In 1942, French peasants sold a third of all their butter, eggs, and pigs on the black market; a quarter of all the potatoes, half of all the chickens. In 1943, of 1,150,000 tons of meat slaughtered in France, the legal market saw only 191,000 tons. Everything went the same way.

Paris became sinister. There had been famine before, and those who had profited from the general woe. But revolutionary Paris in 1793, and even the Paris of the Directory, did not define itself by a few hundred traffickers. It had trembled with civil war. People ate rats in 1871, while the gold of others allowed them to continue their feasting, but besieged Paris was fighting in the suburbs. Between 1940 and 1944, there was nothing of the sort. Apart from one narrow band of society, and outside the times of collective fever, the mollusk-city seemed to have retreated into its shell, reduced to vegetative functions only. The stomach was all—full stomach, empty stomach. Never in its long history, and one rich with brutal inequities too, had Paris known the disgrace of seeing one section of its community prosper under the boot of an invader—tacitly, when it was not actively cooperating in its own plunder—while tens of thousands literally died of hunger.

The enemy was rotting the city.

PARIS AND THE FINAL SOLUTION

I often wondered, drifting off to sleep long after the war was over, why no one thought of killing Rebatet. Lucien Rebatet wrote on June 6, 1942, in *Je Suis Partout*: "I spoke in this paper last winter of my joy at having seen, in Germany, the first Jews with their yellow stars. It would be a much greater joy to see this star in our own Parisian streets where, not three years ago, that execrable race was crushing us under foot."

The tragedy had already been set in motion.

August 20, 1940, two months after the Wehrmacht's entry into Paris, the Garde Française and the Jeune Front, offshoots of the same Fascist movement, organized the first anti-Semitic demonstration of the Occupation by attacking Jewish shops on the Champs-Élysées. The occupying forces had requisitioned a building on the same street for their use. They paraded about in dark shirts, leather belts, and boots. Prefect of Police Langeron noted them as: "Simple trash. The file on them is particularly edifying."

August 29: The obligatory registration of Jews. The Nobel prizewinner and philosopher Henri Bergson, a sick old man in his eighties, found the strength to go to the police station in his dressing gown and slippers. He had decided, as a gesture of solidarity, to keep his conversion to Catholicism secret.

On November 1, all businesses belonging to Jews had to display the fact with a yellow poster: *Entreprise juive.*

The big optician Lissac informed people with a great deal of publicity: "Lissac is not Isaac."

In some Jewish shop windows, with a touching naïveté, stood the photo of a soldier from the 1914–18 war in his trench—the proprietor—displaying his medals; another showed his military citations, along with three members of his family who were veterans of the last three wars against Germany; yet another protested: "We have been French since the seventeenth century." Poor people! Many had counted on Pétain to protect his old soldiers. But Vichy had, with all the racist ardor of the novice, on its own initiative and without German pressure, just issued regulations pertaining to Jews that surprised even Berlin.

The seizure of goods and property began almost immediately under the pretext of Aryanization.

On May 14, 1941, six thousand Jews were summoned to seven different centers in Paris. Most of them came. They were taken to the camp at Beaune-la-Rolande near Orléans, eventually to end up in Auschwitz. The very old-established French Jewish community refused, for the most part, to heed the signs. Those deported to Beaune were poor devils, foreigners or stateless citizens barely scraped clean of the filth of their central European ghetto, jabbering in a barbaric French. Jews who had been French long before Nice and Savoy were French could not envisage themselves being confused with these people.

But on August 20, there was the first roundup in the 11th arrondissement, undertaken by the Paris police. Nearly six thousand men, women, and children were pulled from their beds at four in the morning and taken to Drancy, antechamber of the death camps. This time they were French people.

In September the exhibition entitled "The Jews" opened at the Palais Berlitz. It attracted great crowds, as the exhibition on freemasonry had the year before at the Petit Palais. The film *Le Juif Süss* was showing at cinemas all over Paris. The press spewed out its daily torrent of racial abuse. Georges Montandon, a professor of ethnology, wrote frequent articles and lectures on the theme: "How to recognize Jews." "Facial expression is very animated. Gestures lack control. Muscle tone is deficient. Appearance is neglected." Then he mentioned the nose, of course, and the "watery, prominent eyes." Céline, however, was exasperated by the incurable pro-Semitism of his compatriots, and wrote in *Le Pilori* on October 2: "They love to be close to, strapped to, Jewish assholes; they love being plastered in their dung."

The yellow star was to serve as a brand for human cattle. Compulsory from the age of six, it was described in precise detail by General von Stülpnagel in an order of May 29, 1942: "The Jewish star is a six-pointed star, of the dimension of the human hand, with a black outline. It should be in yellow cloth with the word 'Jew' in black letters. It should be worn clearly visible on the left side of the chest, securely sewn onto the clothing." A footnote added that each Jew, in order to receive three stars, would have to surrender one ticket from his clothing ration. A career officer welcome in the highest circles of Parisian society, General von Stülpnagel found no difficulty in descending to the trivial.

A month later, a new regulation forbade Jews, already excluded from most available jobs, to enter restaurants, tearooms, and bars. They were not allowed to attend theaters, cinemas, concerts, or music halls. They were not permitted to use public telephones. Libraries and museums were closed to them, and also markets and fairs, swimming pools and beaches, exhibitions and racecourses, sportsgrounds and campsites. They were banned from visiting forts and castles. And in the Métro they could only use the last carriage of the train. And last, with a remarkable refinement of cruelty, they were obliged to do their shopping between three and four o'clock in the afternoon, that is to say, when most food shops—their shelves having been long since emptied—had pulled down their metal shutters.

There were fine gestures. What can one say? In a city like Paris you will always find fifty thousand takers for any new idiocy—an exhibition on freemasonry or Jews, say—and a thousand brave souls to keep a conscience. In several schools they made a special fuss of little Jewish children, many of whom had refused to go to school, and had been dragged there in tears by their unhappy parents. Passersby shook hands with complete strangers with stars on, as an expression of solidarity. They did not know then that no one else would ever be able to share the destiny of the Jews, that it would remain forever incommunicable. We learned that a Parisian architect had painted "Auvergnat" on a yellow star that he had made for himself. He was sent to Drancy along with several other Parisians who had worn the yellow star without being entitled to. But they were kept there only for a few weeks; in the rigorous mental categories of racist fascism even volunteers had no right to a Jewish destiny.

The Paris press gave as much column space to the great roundup of July 16–17, 1942, as to the opening of the new cabaret Le Florence. The previous night, *Le Petit Parisien* had written this about the whole round of anti-Semitic measures just taken by the occupying power: "The Jews wanted war. The evil-mindedness of their race has thrown the whole world into this dreadful conflict. Compared with such a crime, the most recent measures against them appear benign." Even the great July 16–17 roundup of twelve thousand Jews did not appease the likes of Céline. Brasillach, soft-soaping, reassured people in *Je Suis Partout* that if any little children had been separated from their parents during the roundup, it must have been the work of agents provocateurs in the police. The Parisian Collaborationist scum did not even feel that bizarre prick of conscience felt by Dutch racists who, at the first roundups, scrawled on the walls of Amsterdam: "Keep your filthy hands off our filthy Jews."

But it would be easy only to have recourse to racist literature to further stigmatize the most tragically memorable event of the four years of the Occupation. The Jews herded into the Vélodrome d'Hiver knew only too well to what extremes racial hatred could push the enemy. But they were not expecting that the first stage of their march to the final torture chamber would take place amid general indifference. (A black irony of fate would have it that the famous photo, seen everywhere, showing them all assembled in the huge stadium, centerpiece of Paris life, was to be identified much later by a learned historian as having been taken in August 1944, when the same Vélodrome d'Hiver was full of those presumed to have been collaborators, for the purposes of interrogation. Which means that for four decades our eyes had inevitably lingered not over the martyrs but over those who had cheered them towards their Calvary.) Survivors were to tell just how cruel their bus journey through an indifferent Paris had been. Twelve thousand of our people disappeared without creating more ripples than a pebble in a pond. Disappearances were not uncommon, it is true. Somewhere a telephone would ring and ring without answer; a door remained obstinately closed. The concierge would murmur: "They have been." As a precaution, you removed their name from your address book. But twelve thousand people at a stroke! I don't remember the slightest attack of collective fever, or even one of those lightning rumors. Galtier-Boissière, Guéhenno, the Groult sisters, Micheline Bood: their diaries do not breathe a word about it. Fabre-Luce, distinguished memoirist, devotes a chapter to "the assassination of the Franc," but not a line to that of the Jews. Collective nonassistance to people in danger? It was impossible to offer help, but we could at least have taken notice of this horrifying spectacle; but we turned our backs on it. The Paris police performed their shameful task; the Vélodrome d'Hiver took in the poor crowd as if they might have been there for the six-day summer festival; the buses trundled towards Drancy as though to some ordinary suburb; the death trains ran on time.

Forty years later, a man my age told me that his mother, a fervent Christian, had been warned about the roundup, rushed to the Vélodrome d'Hiver, and managed to get near the railings. A Jewish woman, jostled by the guards, was able to pass her baby out. No words had been exchanged. There was no hesitation on either side. Women, in such extreme circumstances, are more intelligent. That child, brought up by its adopted family, now plays in the Orchestre de Paris. We know how nearly all the others ended up.

Rebatet died in his bed on August 24, 1972, at Moras-en-Valloire (Drôme), the village of his birth.

STEMMING THE TIDE

The year 1942 was a cruel one. In Asia, the yellow tide seemed unstoppable. In Africa, "the desert fox" Rommel kept up the offensive. In Europe, we watched, astounded and with grudging admiration, as the Wehrmacht not only survived the Russian winter, but, no sooner had the snows melted, forged ahead towards the Don, crushing everything in its path. On August 19, Anglo-Canadian troops landed at Dieppe but were slaughtered or taken prisoner. In the Atlantic, German U-boats sank as many Allied ships as during the two previous years put together.

August 30, 1942, saw Nazi power at its apogee; it took blind faith not to believe in Hitler's victory. Rommel had the Pyramids in his sights. He was twice as close to the Tcherek as to Berlin. The Tcherek, a Caucasus river, was the last obstacle separating von Kleist's army from the oilfields of Baku. On that August 30, at three in the afternoon, the soldiers of the 394th Hamburg armored infantry regiment advanced on the river, 250 meters wide, establishing a bridgehead on the eastern bank, resisting the Soviet counterattack. In the Führer's headquarters at Vinnitsa in the Ukraine, the Nazi marshals were predicting the meeting, somewhere near Baghdad, of Rommel's victorious Afrika Korps and von Kleist's armored advance guard.

We were powerless spectators, watching with bated breath, while our fate hung in the balance.

The balance finally tipped our way in the autumn. Rommel, defeated at El Alamein, began a retreat that would take him right back to Tunis. The francophone German press announced, week after week, the "total conquest" of Stalingrad, then the encirclement by Paulus' "victorious army." The Anglo-Americans wiped out the memory of Dieppe by successful landings in Algeria and Morocco. The Wehrmacht replied with an invasion of Pétain's kingdom, which would have been within reach of the Swiss Army. As in 1941, with the failure of the Germans beneath the walls of Moscow, and the entry of the USA into the war, 1942, after ten cruel months, finished on a note of hope.

Which is why 1943 was the worst year. The war had made us so accustomed to catastrophic collapses that the deadly blows received by the Wehrmacht should have spelled disaster. But if German soldiers no longer had the means to conduct a blitzkrieg, they still jealously guarded the recipe. They struck with thunder; we were taking little bites. Sights would have to be lowered. Neither winter nor spring would be the season of our liberation. After the Allied operations in North Africa, Winston Churchill, the man who never lied, took it upon himself to damp our enthusiasm: "It is not the beginning of the end; it is the end of the beginning." So the landings that would release us could not now take place until the summer, or at worst the autumn.

Paris was changing. The occupation of the so-called Free Zone had closed down the Vichy puppet theater. The mystique of the Maréchal, the old rag with which France covered its nakedness, was torn to tatters in the November winds. Pétain's most fervent followers were loath to admit that he would have jumped on a plane heading for Africa as soon as the announcement was made that Hitler's divisions had crossed the demarcation line. De Gaulle the sword, Pétain the shield; the double symbol appealed to those souls who were disinclined to make difficult choices and who could justify a wait-and-see policy. But if indeed the shield had ever done his job (something which many—notably Anglo-Saxon—historians deny), of what use could he be after November 1942? The Francisque, Pétain's medal, fell from people's buttonholes like autumn leaves.

War seized the city. It came from the skies with Allied air raids on factories working for the enemy, and on train yards. On March 3, 1942, the RAF had plunged Boulogne-Billancourt into mourning: 623 dead, 1,500 wounded. The Renault factory was the target. "I grieve with Paris," Pétain let it be known. Paris was crying tears of rage, but even the outcry against "English barbarism" did not mean that we forgot the Stukas that had bombed the columns of refugees leaving the city in 1940. On April 4, 1943, Renault was attacked again; more than 300 died. On July 14, they picked the northern suburbs. Hardly a week went by from now on without its air-raid warning. The sirens whined several times a day. Onlookers blithely continued to ignore the instructions of the civil defense, choosing to study, noses in the air, the grouping of the squadrons and the precision of the flak. Schoolchildren had no choice but to go to the air-raid shelters, so that the lugubrious wailing of a siren which interrupted a boring lesson would be greeted with shouts of joy. The general atmosphere was one of optimism, despite the crises, because each demonstration of Allied power meant that our liberation was nearer.

You had to know what you wanted. But then, one man whose child was killed by a bomb strangled a complete stranger with his bare hands, just because he happened to be praising de Gaulle. We thought the pilots more than a little inaccurate, but preferred to blame the Americans. Our English remained untainted. Because, whenever we spoke about the Anglo-Saxon Allies, we would always say "the English." America was more nebulous. We had confidence in its arms, but less in its soldiers. Those who landed to liberate us would be "the English." After London and Coventry, the RAF pilots knew just how much damage could be inflicted on civilian populations, and were supposed to take any acceptable risk to limit the carnage. The American Flying Fortresses were less maneuverable than the British bombers, and they used the carpet-bombing technique, which could not target accurately. So we had to mourn our dead and at the same time be pleased that our Allies were strong enough to come and kill them in the first place. Being a conquered people is not easy.

The enemy seized the city. Their French partisans got organized, paraded, and armed themselves. It was no longer the time for ideological debate but for armed struggle. The Légion des Volontaires Français who went to the Eastern Front in the euphoria of those first victories, behaved so badly under fire that their German masters restricted them to repressing the Soviet resistance. Vichy had created the Légion des Combattants, a grotesque organization that aimed to recall veterans and put them at the service of the National Revolution. It was really more stupid than menacing. But Darnand started the Service d'Ordre Légionnaire, recruited among young people, and announced baldly in the pages of a paper called *La Trique* ("The Cudgel"): "You must understand that for us action is a sacred duty and that it will often breed violence." In 1943 the Service d'Ordre, 25,000 strong, became the Militia, "the country's principal instrument of moral, intellectual, social, and political recovery." Darnand filled the Vélodrome d'Hiver with his Militia. Doriot, a member of the Légion des Volontaires Français, addressed packed houses whenever he came home on leave. Bucard, Déat, Fascist party leaders, drilled their men in the streets and held meetings in an endeavor to recapture the joys of the Nüremberg rallies. The statue of Joan of Arc, on the Rue de Rivoli, witnessed the march-past of Fascist cohort after Fascist cohort. Poor Gaudin at the Arc de Triomphe had to hold out the ceremonial sword to the self-styled "leaders" (Bucard, "the leader who has never been wrong," Doriot, "the leader who fights Bolshevism," and Déat, "the leader France needs") who had come to rekindle the flame at the head of their troops. Those of us who saw it with our own eyes were surprised later to see the Collaboration treated as though it were some sort of intellectual wager without stakes which had gone wrong. The Collaboration was jackbooted and armed: it marched down the Champs-Élysées in neat columns; it "corrected" onlookers who were tardy in removing their hats when the banners went by; it put into the streets of Paris a species that no one would have dared to predict in the darkest days of 1940: a French soldier in Nazi uniform with a tricolore badge on the arm like a stain. The Collaboration was not only the highly strung Drieu La Rochelle, the little nobody Brasillach, and the scum Rebatet. It was above all the tens of thousands of bullyboys, recruited by the so-called "leaders" in order to impose terror and gain power.

And the enemy seized the people too. The war effort mobilized all their men, so they needed a workforce from the Occupied countries to slave in their factories. What began as a voluntary exercise, promising the release of one prisoner of war for every three workers, ended up being compulsory, the Service du Travail Obligatoire. It applied to all men between the ages of 18 and 50, and women from 21 to 35.

Because the first callups were more or less obeyed, London and the Resistance had to redouble their efforts, and their warnings were printed on flyers or chalked on the German posters: "A man who leaves is a hostage in enemy hands," "Do not go; it is treason," "If you do not want to die under English bombs, don't go to Germany." As the months went by, defaulters grew in numbers. Those who were eligible to go took cover in jobs in the fire brigade, the police, civil defense, on the railways. Solicitors' clerks chose to go down the mines to escape the Service du Travail Obligatoire. When all the protected jobs got filled, people left for isolated farms in twos and threes, and tens—becoming the embryonic Maquis. But many had to stay in Paris, relying on changes of address and trusting to luck in order to avoid the roundups, because the enemy, under the impetus of the Nazi Ritter, chief slave-trader for France, launched a hunt for the tens of thousands of defaulters in hiding in the city (soon one potential conscript in two would be avoiding callup). This ushered in perhaps the single most drastic change in atmosphere in the capital, much more so than the start of the attacks, with the cycle of reprisals. This time it was a mass action, not just a handful of atypical volunteers, and affected those uncommitted people whose only crime was wanting to escape from an unreasonable demand of war—those previously indifferent people to whom Cardinal Liénart, high dignitary of a Church well and truly under the thumb of Vichy, audaciously declared: "It is not a sin to seek to avoid the Service du Travail Obligatoire."

From then on the roundups were a permanent feature. In the Métro, at cinema exits, in the Latin Quarter, in the working-class districts, cordons of police infiltrated the crowds and arrested anyone whose work permit was not in order. Often, these were sent directly to Germany, without being allowed home to collect their belongings. Workers were the first to be arrested, but students, who had always been exempt, and white-collar workers soon would no longer escape the common fate, which affected all classes of French society. Even those who in 1940 had regretfully declared, "They are right," were playing cat and mouse with the Occupier in 1943.

The Resistance was eating away at the city. Intensification of the armed struggle had gradually changed public opinion. In 1941, the attacks were condemned; in 1943, Parisians raged at the reprisals taken by the enemy. The enemy, overwhelmed, had retaliated by extending punishment to families: "All close male relatives, as well as brothers-in-law and cousins over the age of 18 will be shot; all women similarly related will be sentenced to hard labor; all children up to the age of 17 of those men and women affected by these measures will be sent to an approved school."

Hatred breeds hatred, and assassination attempts increased. In 1943 it was an almost daily event for snipers to fire at the enemy in Paris. Most were Communists, often foreign, veterans of anti-Fascist combat, former members of the International Brigades taking their revenge on the banks of the Seine for defeats suffered on the Spree in Berlin or by the Manzanares in Madrid. Men of iron like Joseph Epstein, alias Colonel Gilles, aged 32 in 1943, hero of the Brigades, joined the French Army in 1939, was imprisoned but quickly escaped, leader of the FTP in the Paris area. To him we owe the memorable operation against the German Champs-Élysées parade which, in the interest of our continuing humiliation, marched up to the Arc de Triomphe every single afternoon. He was insanely daring to attack this symbol of enemy power in broad daylight in an area bristling with police and soldiery. Epstein added tactical genius to audacity. Up till then the partisans had operated in groups of three; one to throw or shoot, and two to provide cover. Once the grenade had been thrown, or the shots fired, it was a question of running for your life with all the German survivors at your heels— the critical phase, capture or death. Epstein mobilized fifteen men. He placed three throwers on the Champs-Élysées. Their grenades made bloody holes in the enemy ranks. The survivors and police escorts gave chase. Three partisans in the first line of defense opened fire, then fell back. A hundred yards farther on, the second line opened fire. A hundred yards farther on, there was a third group. The pursuers, disconcerted by the barrage of successive and unexpected shots, took cover to await reinforcements. The partisans made their escape. Only one was slightly wounded in the hand. All Paris was talking about this masterstroke.

Among Epstein's troops was an élite detachment known as the Manouchian group, and in this group was an eighteen-year-old boy, blond, green-eyed, gentle but with absolute sangfroid. No plaque recalls the name of Marcel Rayman, and no Parisian street or square has ever been deemed worthy of his name. Rayman! He was one of those young Jews who had seen all his family taken away in the roundups of 1942, whose hatred of the Nazis was deep and bitter. Rayman killed the slave-driver Ritter, numerous enemy officers, not to mention traitors and French police in their service, trained his comrades, and led the special international team whose job was to do the impossible.

Between June and October 1943, the Manouchian detachment attacked the enemy every other day. Grenades in requisitioned hotels and restaurants, grenades in troop buses; execution of officers like General von Apt; derailment of trains; attacks on offices of French Fascist organizations; liquidation of Gestapo informers.

The streets started to look different. It was a long time ago that France was the Wehrmacht's brothel, its Capua, its soldiers' rest. Requisitioned hotels, *Soldatenheim*, and *Soldatenkino* were surrounded by sandbags. I watched officers, who once would have marched—heels clacking, caps worn rakishly, uniforms spangled with medals—sneak discreetly out of the Senate headquarters of the Luftwaffe, in civilian clothes. Companies of soldiers moved about only with an advance guard, a rear guard, and a side guard, with automatic pistols trained on passersby. German buses full of troops drove slowly so as not to endanger the sentinels poised on the pavement, ready to fire. The top brass, by contrast, sped along avenues at top speed, flanked by motorcycle outriders, reducing the risks by going fast. At nightfall, it became a rare sight to see uniformed men walking the streets. Even in broad daylight one saw anxiety in the eyes of troops stuck in some unknown district of the city. Fear had not changed camp; it was now present in both camps.

The frightening trial of strength initiated by Fabien on August 21, 1941, was being won. Even if the firing squads at Mont-Valérien were still executing 30 or 50 at a time, the enemy, struggling, was being forced to recognize the guerrillas as a fact. In December 1940, the engineer Bonsergent had been shot for having jostled a German junior officer in the crowd at the Gare Saint-Lazare. Three years later, anyone arrested bearing arms was simply, dare one say, sent to a concentration camp, and the enemy executed half as many hostages in 1943 as in 1942. The partisan terror had made Nazi terror back down.

The Resistance was also three well-dressed men taking a quiet stroll round the lake in the Bois de Boulogne, to all intents and purposes discussing horses or the stock exchange. Instead of splattering the pavements with German blood, these three gentlemen were putting the finishing touches to what would be the future Conseil National de la Résistance. The thin man was André Dewavrin, alias Colonel Passy. His presence in Paris that March 31, 1943, was one of the rashest of many such acts. He was director of the BCRA, de Gaulle's intelligence service. Passy knew all the cells, and the networks—all the secrets. His capture would have had the most incalculable consequences. Once in a while he fiddled with the heavy signet ring which concealed the ultimate safeguard—his cyanide pill.

With him were Pierre Brossolette, who was to throw himself to his death from the window of the Gestapo building in the Avenue Foch rather than talk, and Jean Moulin, who was to die under torture with lips sealed.

Their colleague Rémy, whose career as a film producer had been interrupted by the war, led a life in the intelligence service of the kind you only see in films. By right he ought to have been arrested a hundred times over. Rémy it was who took to London the detailed plan of the Atlantic wall between Le Havre and Cherbourg, before even the first blocks of concrete were laid.

By 1943 the Paris Resistance was no longer something quasi-mythical that people only whispered about. It was made flesh made visible. It struck like lightning when its street fighters went into action. It gathered information; it organized. It inscribed freedom, like a watermark, beneath the surface of the subject city. The pull of the Resistance magnet drew people from diverse social groups and threw them together. A fleeing councillor of state might find himself spending a night in the back of a shoe-mender's shop. Rémy was an old-fashioned Royalist, opposed to Communist guerrillas. But he cemented friendships with several of their number which the worst upheavals of the postwar period could not break.

It was not altruism; the social front would never be confused with the patriotic front. Passy and Rémy, Epstein and Rayman were not fighting for the same future, but they were fighting the same enemy. That was enough.

TORTURE

A sinister Monopoly board: Rue Lauriston, Rue des Saussaies, Avenue Henri-Martin, Boulevard Flandrin, Rue de la Pompe—the haunts of the French Gestapo, otherwise known as *la carlingue*. March 15, 1943: Berlin ordered the closing of the purchasing offices that had been bleeding the French economy dry. Masuy, Lafont, Mérode, Brandl, Berger, and several others whose lairs had always served as covers for the serious business of repression, now put heart and soul into the pursuit of the Resistance fighters. Their efforts were vital, because enemy troops, diminished in numbers by the insatiable Eastern Front, could not manage to stem the rising tide of the Resistance.

Masuy was the inventor of the bath torture, but his preference was for fine work. He had purchased a complete set of surgeon's tools, and if someone refused to talk he would sigh, open his drawer, bring out ten or so bizarre and fearfully sharp little instruments, lay them out on his desk and then ask in a languid voice: "Do you really want to make me use all these?" At Lafont's base, where the team had been picked from among the inmates of Fresnes prison, released on the nod of an obsequious prison governor, Serge Marongin, and Abel Danos, known as the Mammoth, were the best-qualified torturers. Sonia Boukassi, a drug addict, and Violette Morris, onetime French weight-lifting champion, both lesbians, were the chief women's interrogators. Berger, together with 30 or so men and women guilty of black marketeering, who had had to choose between Collaboration and deportation, made up one of the most murderous teams of the lot. His former customs officials, dentists' technicians, chefs, and shopkeepers proved just as ferocious in practice as the worst of Lafont's criminals. They killed 300. No special training or vocation is necessary for the profession of torturer. The interrogations took place on the first floor of 180 Rue de la Pompe, in a spacious bourgeois drawing room complete with wallhangings, Old Masters, deep armchairs, and a superb grand piano on which Zimmer, a former teacher, would play classical music while they burned a woman's fingers or rubbed salt into the cuts on a man's feet. All under the phlegmatic eye of Berger, generally sporting a silk dressing gown. The rules of the house stated that all prisoners, male or female, should be stripped on arrival.

Sadism did its dismal work. Intelligence caused more harm. Lafont, Masuy, and the others knew how best to spin a thick spider's web of accomplices over Paris. At the end of 1943, for each agent of the Abwehr and the Gestapo present in the city, there were 40 or 50 French auxiliaries. It was these people who dealt the most severe blows to the Resistance. They came from all walks of life, knew the ropes, took to it like ducks to water. There was Lafont, and his sidekick, the ex-cop Bonny (once known as "the best policeman in France," before being sacked for corrupt practices), the criminals living off immoral earnings, and a host of countesses and marquises without a mention in the *Almanach de Gotha*. There were ex-army people, workers, journalists, businessmen, civil servants. No trade or state body was spared. At the time of the Liberation, the police officers charged with the inquiry discovered the rottenness to be so far-reaching that they were under orders to close the files, on the debatable grounds that the nation's morale, already severely weakened, would not support the shock of such devastating revelations. "A generalized cancer" was how the officer responsible, Commissioner Clos, described it.

This is how the enemy wanted things to be. They had dragged people like Lafont out from the lowest depths with the deliberate intention of morally subverting French society. "I will turn the war rotten," Hitler had announced. The SS chiefs in Paris, Oberg and Knochen, had applied the law to the letter. Oberg was an austere man, who had the profoundest contempt for Lafont, the common criminal. He made him a *Hauptsturmführer* in the SS and let him parade around in his captain's uniform. He gave him full powers to remove whomever he liked from prison—delinquents, Resistance fighters, Jews, traffickers—in such a way that the powerful debased themselves before Lafont and the weak let themselves be enrolled in order to save a wife or husband. He allowed Lafont, and the others, the right to unrestricted pillage, because he knew, in spite of his own personal integrity, the corrupting power of money.

Two hitherto unknown sides of Paris were locked in mortal combat. The Resistance, thrown together in a provisional union, in which the élite of the future was being forged, and the Collaboration, whose dreams turned to nightmares as the Wehrmacht dissolved away in the Soviet melting pot. This end-of-an-era, twilight atmosphere encouraged unheard-of promiscuities. Furious despair broke down the barriers.

Lafont, a handsome man afflicted with a falsetto voice, onetime pimp turned SS captain, with aspirations to be *préfet*, had made his home in a sumptuous mansion in Neuilly, Rue de Madrid, filled with orchids and dahlias—his great passion. Portraits of Hitler and Goering, 9½ feet square, hung in the entrance hall. Guests were hand-picked: Abetz, the German Ambassador; Knochen from the SS and his staff; Chasseigne, the Vichy Minister; Bussières, the Prefect of Police; Jean Luchaire, the president of a newspaper syndicate and director of *Nouveaux Temps*, who often solicited substantial loans because he had expensive tastes in mistresses.

People of lesser importance were entertained upstairs at Rue Lauriston, while the tortures took place in the basement, or at the One Two Two, the classiest brothel in Paris, which Lafont had practically annexed, and where he gave fabulous banquets for journalists, famous artists, industrialists, society ladies, politicians. Two years earlier, not one among them would have believed the laughable prediction that they would soon be dining with the likes of Lafont. Many would never have envisaged mixing with the animals from the defunct purchasing bureaus. The temptation of the times and the logic of betrayal had set them on the slippery path of crime.

Lafont would dine with Pierre Laval, the head of the government, who addressed him *tu*, then stop off at Rue Lauriston to see how his interrogations were getting on.

The story of this Paris still awaits its Balzac.

LIFE GOES ON

It had to stop. Everything was running out. Rubber, copper, and nickel had disappeared from circulation. People were surprised at the number of utensils and everyday objects thus rendered unobtainable. To buy an electric light bulb, you had to bring in the dead one; an empty bottle for a full one; a used tube of toothpaste for a new one. We children were in charge of collecting old paper. Hairdressers had to save the hair they cut, for what purpose I dread to think. In the mornings on the way to school, I thrilled to the domineering sound my shoes made with their articulated wooden soles. But dust and stones easily got stuck in the grooves, so you had to keep tapping your feet to get them out, as clay court tennis players do today just before serving.

Winters always seemed arctic, though they were never as cold as the record-beating winter of 1940. The lack of fat in our diet made us especially vulnerable to the cold. We were all martyrs to chilblains of the fingers and toes. Colette wrote an article, memorable for its recommendation to wear gold; she swore by its heat-retaining properties. Of course, this was out of the question for ordinary people. More prosaically, I used to slip an old copy of *La Gazette du Patois* under my sweater, and was inseparable from my balaclava until the spring. Lumber jackets and hay boxes made Scandinavians of us all. Some families wore their old ski clothes all winter. A new suit on the black market cost six thousand francs, or the annual salary of a ticket-collector on the Métro. The authorities invented the "national suit," which could be purchased at a regular price in exchange for two worn-out suits. People could only speculate as to the exact content of the cloth used. The popular singer René Paul made the whole of Paris laugh with the song about his "Pure wool poplar" suit, whose trousers turned into shorts in a rain shower.

Food became even more scarce. We steered a miserable course between the days "without" (three days a week were without meat), and the ration tickets which were not honored. There were fewer and fewer consignments of fresh produce. Mistinguett would cheekily interrupt her song *Je cherche un milliardaire* at the Casino de Paris, to whisper sotto voce, "I'm also looking for a leg of lamb," would give her address, and what's more get her Sunday joint. But we could not all be Mistinguett. For the rest of us, the end was near.

Paradoxically, commerce was booming, although there was less and less to sell. In 1935, 10,266 businesses failed, only 439 in 1944. Official liquidations dropped from 2,222 in 1937 to 48 in 1943. The BOF(*beurre, oeufs, fromage*—butter, eggs, cheese) was cock of the walk.

Smokers suffered too. Parents tried to persuade their children, when they reached eighteen, to let them use their tobacco cards. Street vendors proliferated, selling peculiar cigarettes illicitly. Alternative substances were tried—but then there was hardly a product without its ersatz in those dire days. Some people smoked jerusalem artichoke, others preferred nettles. Nearly everyone possessed an airtight tin whose precious contents, saliva-soaked nicotine-rich cigarette butts, could be reused thanks to a little cigarette-rolling machine. Cigarette ends thrown away in the street never burned unseen. Walking down the Boulevard Saint-Michel one day, my father noticed a dignified old gent quickly bend down to pick one up from the gutter. He was the Appeals Court judge before whom my father was about to plead a case. My father turned away, too late, and was recognized as the old man stood up. He knew immediately that his case was as good as lost.

The barter system held sway. The government put an official stamp on it by, for example, valuing a liter of wine at 200 grams of copper, which emptied certain kitchens of their ancestral cooking pots in the twinkling of an eye. The poorest folk surrendered their modest possessions in exchange for their daily bread, but the better-off came too, because money was by this time a more common commodity than food. Roger-Ferdinand scored a great hit with his play, *Les J3* (in ration-card terms this meant young people between the ages of thirteen and twenty-one), a hilarious comedy in which a group of schoolchildren raised a pig at the back of their classroom and transformed their lycée into a joyful market where everything from silk stockings to batteries could be traded.

There was a definite undercurrent of gaiety in the air in the spring of 1943. In February, the surrender of Paulus and his besieged army at Stalingrad tolled the knell for the Wehrmacht. Even a Goebbels was powerless to diminish the scale of the disaster by the artifice of propaganda. Instead, Berlin chose to dramatize the event by declaring three days' national mourning. On May 12, the Axis troops capitulated at Tunis, including Rommel's legendary Afrika Korps; 250,000 prisoners of war were taken. In the East, the great retreat had begun. The certainty of German defeat made patriotic hearts rejoice, and soothed our stomachs with promise. It was really only the Collabos who were worried. The least political of Parisians knew that famine would last as long as the war did; every step back the Germans took brought the end of our penance nearer.

The streets came to life again with groups of cyclists worthy of the Tour de France, by virtue of their density if not their speed. There were 2 million bicycles for 3 million Parisians. Everyone was at it. A new bicycle cost the same as a prewar car, but the "D" system—make-do-and-mend system—worked wonders somehow or other with the repair of ancient machines found rusting in cellars. A certain celebrated hospital consultant visited his private patients by bicycle, followed at a respectful distance by his valet, balancing the professional bag of tricks in his basket.

Disparate clusters pedaled amid a veritable forest of white signposts (often with black gothic script heavy with exclamation marks) pointing the way in German to the headquarters, barracks, hospitals, "other ranks clubs," offices, and such establishments as the forty brothels reserved for the troops: an enemy sign system grafted onto our own.

I remember how beautiful women were, their legs painted to make up for the missing stockings, their heads topped with extravagant hats, as though they were compensating for the enforced modesty of their clothes by their insane headgear. Paris briefly laughed with the enemy when a German officer wittily remarked to an elegant woman wearing a dizzying hat: "What would it have been like if you had won the war?" The *zazous* brought a note of fantasy to the proceedings. And what tirades there were in the Collaborationist press against those poor *zazous*! Anyone would have thought they threatened the New Order every bit as much as the "Judeo-Bolsheviks" or the "agents of the plutocracy." They were just a group of regular good-for-nothings who hung around a few bars (notably the Pam-Pam on the Champs-Élysées, which was their headquarters), met in cellars to dance the swing (dance halls being out of bounds), and scandalized people with their style of dress—destined for a surprising resurrection forty years later (large loose jackets for boys, square-shouldered jackets for girls, narrow trousers or very short skirts). The Militia persecuted them, and we were only too delighted when Louis Thierry, French boxing champion and *zazou* to boot, knocked a few of them out, just as we were thrilled at the punch-to-fell-an-ox that Jean Marais laid on the journalist Alain Laubreaux from *Je Suis Partout*, who had referred to Cocteau as a "degenerate simpleton."

Montparnasse, for so long the fashionable place to be, gave way to Saint-Germain-des-Prés.

The theater was as lively as ever, and the cinema, and books, but the spirit was no longer the same. Not without malice, after the war, survivors of the Collaboration were keen to lump together all those "who had been published during the Occupation." It was a summary kind of amalgamation. Although there is no doubt either that the citizens of the republic of letters had not shown themselves as a group to be endowed with exemplary greatness of spirit. Parisian publishers had accepted the "Otto list" of September 28, 1940, with perfect docility, pulping 842 Jewish or anti-Fascist authors whose work had been condemned to obscurity. (On return to school in October that year, schoolchildren discovered history books with pages stuck together, and those choosing to study German—suddenly it was three times more popular than English—would find written at the foot of a text by the Jewish writer Heinrich Heine, *Unbekannter Dichter*—"Anon."). The mania to be published, to have his name in the reviews, led more than one writer into excesses of the worst kind.

The law of the jungle. It regulated every kind of behavior right up till the eve of the Liberation. But over and above individual behavior, the evidence points to the fact that we did not read with the same eyes in 1943 as in 1940. When Montherlant wrote his *Solstice de juin*, a celebration of the triumph of pagan-Fascism over "Judeo-demo-crassy," it was at a time when Hitler's victory seemed assured and someone like Heine destined for total eradication. When he staged *La Reine morte* in 1942 at the Théâtre-Français, the audience applauded wildly at the following lines, "We kill, and the skies clear," which seemed like a justification of the assassinations, as did "the flower of our nation is in prison." The author had not changed—he was still equally vain and pusillanimous—but while his *Solstice* shared some of the characteristics of our abasement, and legitimized it, two lines in his play, doubtless without his having intended so, fanned the flames of hope. Sartre's play *Les Mouches* was justifiably received by the public as a hymn to freedom, just as in Anouilh's *Antigone* people applauded the heroine's unshakable resolve, while Créon, the "yes" man, who declared, "I know I have dirty work to do," was even more easily identified with Laval because the director had togged out his henchmen in the leather greatcoats we saw on Gestapo agents.

But the saving grace of 1943 was the very fact of being able to read and go to the theater or cinema without having to suffer too many pangs of conscience. In the early years, when the enemy seemed unbeatable, every new work came to us smeared with the filth of events, and we responded with raw sensibilities. In 1943, artistic endeavor was judged more for what it was. Born of necessity in the dunghill of the Occupation, we knew that art, if it was good, would be destined to bloom in the sunshine of our forthcoming freedom.

There was thus a certain lightheartedness which, in some quarters, approached bad taste. When Allied bombers attacked Billancourt on April 4, 1943, several bombs fell on the racecourse at Longchamp, which was reopening. There were seven dead and many wounded. The bodies were removed, the track modified to avoid the craters, and the racing restarted. "This fact alone indicates the extent of our debasement," wrote Jean Guéhenno in his *Journal*. Perhaps. Three years before, the same people would have thrown themselves in a ditch with their hearts in their mouths the moment a black speck, which might have been a crow or a Stuka, appeared in the sky.

There were half as many suicides in 1943 as there had been in 1940.

Still no reason for it not being high time to stop!

THE TIDE TURNS

But it was still not over. In July and August the Allied Navy had sunk 90 German U-boats, forcing Doenitz to withdraw his submarine fleet from the Atlantic to try and improve the vessels. In the Pacific, the Marines hopped from island to island, recapturing them as they went. In the East, the Soviets were advancing slowly but surely—but what a vast area the Ukraine was! The Americans had conquered or liberated Sicily in July. This marked the fall of Mussolini, to our great glee, because if the Führer more than deserved our hatred, Il Duce had never merited more than contempt. No one would forgive him for stabbing in the back, in June 1940, a France already on its knees. Then the English landed in Calabria, on the toe of Italy; the Americans at Salerno, south of Naples. But Hitler responded by sending thirty German divisions to Italy. Where on earth did he get these reinforcements? Would this seemingly inexhaustible Wehrmacht ever run out of men? It dragged on and dragged on. Old folk felt we were back in the 1914–18 war, with all this "patrolling on a calm front," and the trumpeting of an advance of a few hundred yards.

We hung on every word the BBC broadcast. Its voice, jammed by the enemy, had first forbidden us to give up, and had then rekindled our hopes. It was wonderful when Churchill spoke to us in French with such a peculiar accent that our tears became mingled with laughter. De Gaulle, severe, exhorted us with a voice of iron. He was, it turned out, more uplifting to us than to his agents leaving on missions. He was the *non* man par excellence. He spoke to us of a France we could only imagine with our eyes closed. How I loved him! Maurice Schumann made us tremble every evening. The

BBC was so essential that the Vichy government banned the sale of radios on March 31, 1943!

But we wanted more from the BBC than reasons to hope; we needed something definite. Instead of which, the wireless betrayed our confidence. We heard Churchill announcing in the middle of summer: "Before the leaves fall, the Germans will be attacked on new fronts, and battle will rage in the south, the west and the north." Churchill, the man who had never lied to us, who had always refused to coat the pill. It was as clear as day: the south meant Italy, the north doubtless Scandinavia, the west was us, or Belgium, or Holland, which all came down to the same thing. The decisive landing. *The* landing.

The leaves turned russet, then fell. The Allies were still held up north of Naples; German soldiers tanned themselves in the autumn sunshine on their blockhouses of the Atlantic Wall.

The first frosts froze our hearts. We would have to hold on for at least another six months. Pessimists—or were they not simply realists—scoffed: "The Wall has frightened them. They will never come." We did not know whom to believe, now that even Churchill had lied to us.

History would tell us that he had commented openly, but to a select group, that "in war, the truth must be hidden by clouds." His deliberate lie was all part of a planned deception. Because they could not open up the real Second Front so desperately needed by Stalin in 1943, the Allied chiefs of staff had decided to relieve the pressure on the Red Army by simulating a landing and pulling as many German divisions as possible westward. Secret agents were parachuted in with a mission to announce to their networks that the big operation would take place in September; they knew these networks to be particularly thoroughly infiltrated by the enemy, and also that the probable capture of the agents by the Gestapo would lead inevitably to tortures and confessions. The enemy believed in the September landings, but so did Resistance Paris, because the various organizations were buzzing with the news. So, in addition to the general deception, the activists had the impression of having been cruelly cheated.

For the last two years, history had played Father Christmas, tipping a sackful of good news down our freezing chimneys. But this Christmas, the sack was full of promises which turned out to be as worthless as our ration tickets.

The following months were dreadful. The Resistance was being throttled to death. Historians of the period established later that life expectancy had never been shorter for a member of the Resistance than during the first months of 1944. The enemy was reaping the benefits of its policies: The *carlingue*, constantly reinforced, proved itself devastatingly effective, culling the networks and infiltrating organizations hitherto inviolate. Their task was simplified by the fact that many cells had cut down on their security in the certain knowledge of the autumn landings. The torture chambers were never empty. In the provinces, the Militia were massacring the Maquis. In Paris they set up flying tribunals that would arrive at Fresne or La Santé prison complete with 10 or 20 coffins, and would haul 10 or 20 poor bastards out of the cells and shoot them no sooner had they stepped before the judge-executioner's bench. It was enough to make you weep with rage. To have held out for two or three years, sometimes more, and then to die needlessly when perhaps deliverance was at hand. The Russians were forging ahead as never before. They had pushed beyond their 1940 frontiers, into Rumania, Poland, and Czechoslovakia. We ended up feeling that even if the others never did land, the Russians would finish the job all on their own. But each one of us, inside the walls of our own solitude, felt like a pawn in the game being played, against the clock, between Zhukov's tanks and death itself.

On February 21, Marcel Rayman, Missak Manouchian, and 21 of their comrades were executed by firing squads at Mont-Valérian. As with the "trial of the 27" in April 1942 (when 25 were shot), which was filmed by the Propagandastaffel, the enemy wanted a spectacular trial for the Manouchian group. The walls of the city were plastered with huge red posters denouncing the "army of crime." Did the Nazis hope to frighten people by throwing these death's-head photographs of foreigners at us? Who else were we expecting to save us if not foreigners? Aragon spoke the truth in his immortal poem; anonymous hands wrote graffiti beneath those portraits which read like heartrending sobs.

But there was another poster that did hit the mark. It showed a snail creeping slimily up the boot of Italy, with English and American flags on its shell, with this phrase, "It's a long way to...Rome!," an ironic echo of the traditional "It's a long way to Tipperary," which many hummed in 1940 or 41 when they passed a *feldgrau* in the street. After the Allies had been marking time in Italy for eight months, Juin's Franco-Arab regiments finally managed to break through at Monte Cassino, but poring over our maps, we realized that Italy had a whole mountainous backbone rich with potential stumbling blocks. And the Germans announced the construction farther north of a Gustav Line as solid as the Atlantic Wall.

There was neither bottleneck nor wall to hinder Allied air power. The pilots were working overtime. Pulling out all the stops. But even their most ardent supporters found this kind of zeal a bit excessive. In one single day they left 600 dead in Lyon and 870 in Saint-Étienne; 1,976 the following day in Marseille; and of course thousands of wounded. The squadrons flew over Paris on April 21. They were targeting the station at La Chapelle. They killed 641. Over the airwaves of Radio Paris ("Radio-Paris lies ...Radio-Paris lies...Radio-Paris is German," they sang on the BBC), Philippe Henriot vented his spleen against the "terrorist bombardments" with a damaging eloquence. Pétain came up to Paris for the funeral ceremony, surrounded by German cars. It was his first and last visit during the Occupation.

On May 10, the authorities, without explanation, requisitioned all dogs more than 18 inches tall at the shoulder. This measure caused panic in many peaceful homes. Cautious couples, who had studiously avoided taking any risks to date, experienced the angst of canine concealment, and lived in fear of denunciation by the concierge. No one ever knew why dogs were treated as token Jews. One rumor asserted that the Germans wanted to train the poor beasts to run under tanks with a dynamite charge strapped to their backs.

The cinemas were showing a film about the Atlantic Wall. And it was hard not to be depressed. The footage revealed a formidable blockhouse structure studded with gun emplacements and flame-throwers. In the most impressive sequence, gigantic lifts speed up, in seconds, from the concrete bowels of the building to disgorge several hundred soldiers at a time. Optimists reminded us that films of the same ilk had, in 1939, glorified the impregnable Maginot Line, which had of course stopped absolutely nothing. Pessimists replied that if the Germans had avoided the Maginot Line by going through Belgium, then the Allies would be trying hard to find a weak point in the Wall, which, as enemy propaganda kept telling us, surrounded "fortress Europe" from the North Cape to the Pyrenees.

The Germans changed their propaganda tune, and the new emphasis added to the mute anguish of that spring, when everything seemed to be in suspense. They did not conceal the retreat of the Wehrmacht in the East, but calmly stated that it was a question of "exchanging space for time"—the time to put the finishing touches to secret weapons that would guarantee the Reich a spectacular and final victory. Half a century, or nearly, later, the most difficult thing to do is to explain that our certainty that Hitler would be defeated remained inseparable, until the very last day, from a needling doubt. It remained despite common sense and all the evidence. A glance at the map should have been enough to dispel it. But it would reappear, refusing to vanish altogether, like the one little cloud in a perfect summer sky. For three years we had been able to judge the breathtaking worth of the German soldier in action, but we kept in mind also the Germans' technical mastery of the first stages of the war. The enemy had invented the Blitzkrieg, the armored divisions advancing under cover of Stuka fire, the parachutists dropping in the thousands, the fleets of U-boats. They kept on producing ever more tanks and planes even though Allied bombs had left Germany in ruins. Their engineers could solve any problem. We had seen them survive too many disasters to doubt their indomitable vitality at this stage. Why should a people who knew how to push each individual to his limit, from simple soldier to violent criminal, not also be able to muster men of genius? And if the "miracle weapon" beloved of their propaganda ever got off the drawing board, what would become of us?

The Landing was in the air though. We could tell by the ever-increasing numbers of Allied bombers in the Paris sky. We were spending at least half the school day down in the shelters. One day in May, I saw three Flying Fortresses destroyed by flak at the same time. The remainder of the squadron continued their mission undeterred, their blind determination in the face of danger giving the impression that destiny marched across the skies.

We knew the Landing was in the air because of the increase in "personal messages" transmitted by the BBC to the Resistance. We listened religiously to these enigmatic fragments of weighty baroque poetry. "The moon is full of green elephants" may well have referred to airborne operations, but "Venus has a pretty navel," "The hippo is not carnivorous," "Thérèse is always sleepy"? Without being able to make head or tail of them, we assumed it meant that something was happening.

And then we trustingly thought that they would come because we just could not go on any longer. There was absolutely nothing left. We had thought we had reached the end so many times, yet the finish line kept on moving farther back. Supplies ran out. Rail and road links were cut one after the other by the Allied planes. Vegetables disappeared from the markets. Cooking posed a problem because gas was available

only at mealtimes, and then there was hardly any of it. It was a question of setting up communal kitchens in each district. Power cuts were incessant. Half the Métro stations were permanently closed. Feverishly the enemy increased roundups. You had only to be caught outside the cinema without your papers to be bundled without a trial into a cattle truck bound for Germany.

The city had reached the point of no return.

Why was I not in class on the morning of Tuesday June 6? I cannot remember.

Three windows were flung open simultaneously on the Rue Herschel, where my room gave, and two women and a man yelled in unison: "The English have landed!"

PARIS FALLS APART

So freedom had a foothold in France. All we needed now was a little patience. If there was one virtue we had learned, it was patience. On June 16, the Collaborationist press and radio announced with great gusto that the first of the secret weapons was now in active use: the V1, the pilotless plane, the flying bomb, the meteor packed with dynamite. They said it was invulnerable to anti-aircraft attack, too fast for English fighters. This was the second great test of London, and its defenses would be powerless to repel the attack. Berlin was already announcing the coming of the V2, faster yet, more murderous still. The V3 would spell death for England. *Le Cri du Peuple*, Collaborationist newspaper, was quick to capitalize: "They used to write Vs on the walls. Now write V1, V2, V3 ...." We held our breath. Churchill reassured us: There were only 2,000 dead in London, and life went on. We breathed again. They would hold fast. It had been close.

On June 28, the Resistance executed Philippe Henriot in his ministerial office. What a commotion! He was the first high-ranking traitor to be assassinated in Paris. Laval declared: "Because they had no answer to Philippe Henriot, they have killed him; because they could not shut his mouth, they have shut his eyes." It was almost up to Henriot's standards. A considerable crowd came to pay homage to his mortal remains. Vichy decreed that there would be a state funeral and promised a reward of 20 million francs to anyone catching the killers. The last enemy mouthpiece was therefore Jean Herold-Paquis, a dry little man who spoke in imperious tones, and had been making us laugh for the last six months by winding up his editorials from Radio-Paris with the stock phrase: "And England, like Carthage, will be destroyed!" The V1s, it is true, had wiped the smile off our faces. But Herold was too much of a clown, and the Propagandastaffel decided to repeat the broadcasts of the now-deceased Henriot. So for many weeks Paris listened to Collaborationist propaganda from the lips of a specter. The symbol was an encouraging one.

We learned by word of mouth of the horrifying massacre of the entire population of Oradour-sur-Glane by the Germans, which was not reported in any organ of the press.

The city was cracking. Our faces were permanently tense, though our daily activities remained routine. We all felt under a stay of execution. The Allies were being a bit slow, but would surely soon break out from their all too narrow beachhead. So there would be a battle for the liberation of Paris. Our hearts leaped at the prospect of that liberation, but the thought of the fighting made us quail. Hitler would not be doing us any favors. We knew Caen was in ruins; were we going to be the German Stalingrad?

The Collaborators, devastated by the assassination of Henriot, no longer slept in their own beds. Nearly all of them would by now have received their miniature coffins, or their death warrants in red ink, through the mail.

The city was falling apart. One hour of gas a day. Electricity cut off. Hairdressers put their clients out on the pavement to dry their perms in the sun. The more upscale salons hired the services of cyclists whose robust calf muscles charged the dynamos running the dryers. Theaters played with their roofs open, because the lighting did not work, or with the help of car headlights and candles.

Georges Mandel, onetime Minister of the Interior, freed by the Nazis in Vichy, was killed by the Militia in revenge for Henriot. *Je Suis Partout* commented: "It is certainly deplorable that Mandel the Jew, who deserved death a hundred times over for having pushed France into the war, was not publicly tried and executed. But the essential thing is that Mandel the Jew is no more."

The superb weather showed off women to their best advantage. Read the accounts of that lull before the storm: Resistance and Collaborators, whose perspectives could not have been more different, agreed on one thing: the wonderful legs of Parisian girls. Light, full skirts were in fashion. They billowed up most attractively to reveal the tanned thighs of cyclists, and sometimes the updraft of a passing German truck would blow them right over their heads. I was just thirteen and felt life held great promise.

July 20. Fever again. German tanks took up positions round the principal requisitioned hotels. Troops patrolled, or set up roadblocks. The Place Beauvau was particularly animated. What was going on? We had no idea. The mystery was cleared up with the announcement of the assassination attempt against Hitler, but it was not until very much later that we discovered what had really been happening. The Parisian Wehrmacht conspirators had overpowered the SS forces without firing a shot, then thought better of it on learning of the Führer's miraculous survival. A night's drinking was sufficient to reconcile the enemy brothers. But Hitler did not take the same view. Ten or so superior officers including Stülpnagel, either committed suicide, or were ignominiously hanged.

Marcel Déat wrote in *L'Oeuvre* that the "invaders" were "trapped in a bottleneck" at their beachhead. But then, on July 25, Patton broke through at Avranches, and pushed his tanks across Brittany. Déat then wrote, "This is because it is the only way open to them," showing just how much fear or fanaticism can unbalance a college-trained mind.

We were starving. We had been saying that for four years, but the menus of 1943 now appeared positively sumptuous. Several provinces were in a state of insurrection. Trains no longer ran. Allied planes pounded the roads. A few dozen trucks ferried in all the provisions for the capital of France. They carried a white flag. On the front fenders, two lookouts lying on their backs held one end of a piece of string, whose other end was attached to the driver's arm. As soon as a bomber appeared in the sky, the lookouts pulled on the string. The driver would slam on the brakes, and the whole lot would often as not end up in the ditch. Losses were so frequent that volunteers were becoming scarcer by the day. Fights broke out constantly outside food shops. Riot was in the air.

The enemy was panicking. Official cars tore around the street. Thick smoke belched continuously from the chimneys of the big hotels. Trucks full of troops trundled across the city on their way to the front. They were camouflaged under thick bunches of foliage, so that they looked like the latest production of *Macbeth*. A delivery man caused great mirth throughout the city by decking out his little carrier-bicycle with branches. The *feldgrau* contemplated all this with dull eye, showing no reaction. Packed into vehicles heading for death, they were driven like cattle past the café terraces crammed with chattering customers, their unseeing eyes barely registering the groups of pretty girls walking happily back from the Bois de Boulogne. On foot they looked pathetic. We no longer recognized the splendid specimens of humanity who had paraded for so long up and down our avenues. The battle in Normandy dragged gray-haired old men into Paris, and lanky young boys, dwarves, bandy-legs, hunchbacks—a whole army of ragged men. They reeked of disaster. And with my newfound maturity, I wondered if I had not been a bit unjust to those of our people whom I had seen running away in 1940. A victorious army is always a fine sight. And defeat makes people ugly.

On the Champs-Élysées, the Normandie cinema had posters up for *La Vie de plaisir*.

One afternoon as I was passing the military college-turned-hospital, a convoy of several dozen German ambulances drew up, one behind the other. All at once the war had arrived. The drivers were utterly exhausted. On stretchers in the ambulances, their hastily applied bandages soaked in blood, lay wounded men, most of whom could only have been three or four years older than I was. Some were crying, their faces racked with pain. The heat was so intense that the windows were down. A lament rose from the convoy, the mingling of a hundred moanings, sobbings, and hoarsely murmured cries, which was an even more overwhelmingly strange thing than the sight of these very young men rolling their heads in agony on their stretchers. I owe it to truth to say—knowing that it will not be understood—that the temptation to feel sorry for them did not cross my mind. They would have cheerfully shot my parents. They had to die in order that we could live. I suppose that I would react otherwise today. Childhood is pitiless.

The Paris Resistance desperately sought arms. A German agent, a specialist in infiltration, took advantage of this to lead 35 young people into a trap. Twenty of them were Communists from the FTP, seven belonged to the Jeunesse Chrétienne Combattante, the others to the OCM. Berger's squad, the jewel in the *carlingue* collection, drove them by truck to the fountain in the Bois de Boulogne. They were ordered to jump out one at a time. Despite their pleadings and cries of horror—they were largely adolescents—the executioners fired 35 times.

All over Paris the enemy were packing their bags, burning their files, blowing up their ammunition dumps, and piling their most treasured spoils into trucks. We saw open-topped motorcars speeding eastwards carrying bemedalled generals and glamorous women, and simple soldiers pushing wheelbarrows full of sewing machines. Sightseers gathered in front of requisitioned buildings to savor the spectacle. Collaborators were naïvely surprised to read so much hatred in their eyes; living in clover, they had lost contact with the real world. Several times, exasperated *feldgrau* fired into the crowd. Their nervousness grew as the front edged closer. The Americans had reached Le Mans and Chartres.

Nothing at all worked anymore. Trains and the Métro had all broken down. Provisions—there were none. Then the Post Office went on strike, as well as undertakers. We saw families moving their dead in handcarts. The Paris police, exceptionally, also went on strike. No newspapers were printed, but the Resistance still put up posters.

And on August 19, the uprising broke out.

THE PARIS UPRISING

The unimaginative demonstrated tirelessly and with irrefutable logic that the insurrection was pointless. In fact it made no more sense than the storming of the Bastille. Militarily, the game was up. If most of the Wehrmacht decided to evacuate it would be to avoid being surrounded, and not because of pressure from the Resistance popguns. Politically, the game was up. No faction or party entertained any crazy illusions about imposing power by force. Yet Parisians risked death at the drop of a hat on the very eve of a Liberation they had spent four years waiting for. (Does it not epitomize the history of the Resistance? All over Occupied Europe, men and women perished for acts that were cruelly meaningless when taken individually but which as a whole ended up making sense.) But it was not really about impressing the world with a hastily colored tableau, an *image d'Épinal*, nor about wounding the enemy with what would amount to a pinprick compared to the dreadful wounds they were by then receiving. It was to do with the rest of us. It was a matter between us and our long humiliation. A battle lasting a few days would never wash the city clean of its corruption, but at least the fighters could hold their heads up high, all the more so because they would have fought for the principle of it. Symbolically, the uprising started at the Prefecture of Police, among precisely those who had been for so long the docile henchmen of the enemy, the Jew-hunters and Resistance-trackers, and the first rounds of machine-gun fire came from the window of the Commissioner David's office, whose sinister brigade had patiently tortured the Manouchian gang. Call it opportunism? Last minute volte-face? It was well and truly superfluous. The most deeply compromised, like David and his men, had fled with the enemy or had gone into hiding, and the police as a body knew perfectly well that no power could risk being without their support. The anointing oil of danger would wipe away the marks of submission from their heads, for too long bowed down.

On the eve of deliverance came insane heroisms, of the kind reserved for desperate causes. A Paris already warmed by the rising sun of freedom battled like the Warsaw ghetto. Little kids rushed at Tiger tanks brandishing petrol bombs, men armed with shotguns stopped trucks full of SS, women were shot down trying to retrieve a fallen soldier's automatic pistol.

There were a few people, however, who did not let common sense fly out the window. Several honorable Resistance leaders, Nordling the Swedish Consul, and von Choltitz, the German General who, without being quite the white knight he has been called, had no wish to go down in history as Paris' answer to Nero. A truce was declared on

August 20. The German garrison would be allowed to evacuate Paris without harassment as long as they did not attack anyone on their part. The fact was that the Prefecture of Police, on the evening of August 19, had only two hours' worth of ammunition left. Choltitz, with his relatively large amounts of fire power, hesitated to start a battle that might have an unpredictable outcome. Good sense suggested a truce. But good sense was all about being a supporter of Pétain in 1940, a wait-and-see in 1941 and 1942, a cautious Gaullist in 1943, and a more resolute Gaullist in 1944. The insurrection was all about sweeping away four years of good sense. The entirely reasonable truce, immediately contested by the most dedicated Resistance members, went against the irresistible wave of opinion which was about to burst over the city. Even before anyone knew anything about the arguments it was causing in the various headquarters, the guns started firing all on their own.

The suburbs organized themselves around their recaptured town halls. In Paris itself the main thrust of the fighting was along the Boulevard Saint-Michel, which the Germans made every effort to keep open by launching armored attacks from the Jardin du Luxembourg, one of their strongholds. But there was fighting in nearly every quarter of the city. Skirmishes, furtive sniping, rapid retreats to escape the lightning reactions of the Germans. Cars painted with the Cross of Lorraine prowled the streets, two gunners on the front fenders in the manner of Spanish Republicans. From his command post at Denfert-Rochereau, in the heart of the catacombs, Colonel Rol-Tanguy, military commander of the Paris FFI, tried desperately to pull together the threads of the battle.

Joliot-Curie organized a production line of Molotov cocktails in his laboratory at the Collège de France. Weapons were scarce.

The walls were already liberated. Violent posters called on people to fight. Coldly technical texts explained the best way to immobilize tanks. The Germans, however, had stuck scary reminders across these: "*Achtung!* Be warned. The fate of Paris is in your hands."

The swing from violence to calm and back again was most extraordinary. A peaceful street could be bloodied by a brief skirmish; then, once the wounded had been removed and the blood washed away, people would bring their chairs back out onto the pavement and pick up their conversations where they had left off. The Pont de la Concorde was being raked by gunfire while a few yards below on the banks of the Seine dozens of swimmers were lying sunbathing. On August 23, in the thick of the battle, a painter set up his easel at the dangerous Observatoire crossroads, with the Senate in the background and the Boulevard Saint-Michel swarming with armored cars, and painted all morning, without a care in the world. A few hundred feet from the Hôtel-de-Ville, occupied by the Resistance, and attacked ten times by Tiger tanks, tranquil fishermen trolled their lines in the Seine. Everywhere there were ten onlookers for every fighter and for each fallen fighter 50 people waiting to use his weapon.

On August 21, Resistance newspapers were published openly for the first time. You cannot understand what they signified for us. We read in black and white things that had only been whispered for four years. There were glorious headlines, military communiqués, editorials, but also advice for users of gas appliances. And even helpful hints for families. We could believe in freedom when it got down to everyday matters.

On August 22, the paving stones themselves rose up. No doubt a unique example of a city rewriting its past, Paris drew its genius from the lessons of history. The city bristled with barricades. At least fifty on the first day, two or three hundred on the next. Some were essential, like the huge barricade raised at the intersection between the Boulevard Saint-Michel and the Boulevard Saint-Germain. Many others were constructed in sidestreets where no German soldier would have dreamed of venturing, but were maintained with all the care and attention that might be lavished on a work of art. The imaginary past materialized; photographic images converged with *images d'Épinal*, as each one who enthusiastically pulled up the cobblestones knew, by scientific certainty or by some obscure collective memory, that he was reproducing the very same gestures as those made in 1830, 1848, 1871. It was, however, the first time in the history of Paris that police and rebels were fighting on the same side of the barricades.

The enemy retained its capacity for damage and destruction. The Germans set fire to the Grand Palais, kept up the massacre of prisoners. No barricade could have resisted a tank charge, not even the one in the Rue Saint-Jacques which was decorated with photos of Hitler, Mussolini, and Goering removed from the Italian bookshop on the Boulevard Saint-Germain. But the simple multiplication of obstacles would have posed them a problem. In the Rue de Rivoli, there were six barricades in the space of a half-mile, another six on the Boulevard de la Chapelle, five more between Nation and République. Like Gulliver held down by stone manacles, the enemy retrenched in their strongholds: Senate and Luxembourg, Opéra, École Militaire, the barracks in République and Clignancourt, among other places. They no longer recognized their Paris. The miserable weapons of the patriots worried them less than their sheer numbers, and their numbers less than their fearsome physiognomies. "Delinquents," as Choltitz kept on saying. The prospect of falling into their hands was a sobering thought for the officers at the Ritz and the Majestic headquarters.

The leaders of the uprising had other worries. Knowing themselves to be short of arms, they knew they could not reduce the number of German operation bases. A concerted offensive by the enemy with armored cover would have meant a massacre. The most alarming rumors were going around. Two SS divisions were about to return to Paris. The bombers based at Le Bourget were preparing a massive attack. The Luftwaffe had built a succession of underground bunkers beneath their Senate headquarters; people were saying they were packed with enough explosives to destroy the whole area.

Rol-Tanguy, who had refused to accept the truce, remained a realist. The day after the uprising, August 20, he had sent his chief of staff Gallois-Cocteau through the enemy lines to ask the Allies for help and assistance. After many mishaps he met Patton during the night of August 21–22. The American General told him straight out that his plan of action did not include a march on Paris. The Allies would surround the city, then pursue their advance eastwards, overcoming German resistance as they came to it. For Rol's emissary, this signaled the certainty of a massacre of the insurgents. Devastated, he asked if it would be possible to meet Leclerc, legendary commander of the 2nd armored division. He was given permission. Leclerc was under orders from Bradley. On the evening of the 22nd, Bradley gave the French General the go-ahead.

It was the salvation and probably also the historical justification of the uprising. Without it, Choltitz and his 20 thousand men, with freedom of movement, with their forces intact, would have seen themselves hemmed in by regular troops fighting a traditional war. There is no doubt that they would have joined battle. And a hundred precedents indicate that it would have been murderous and destructive.

LIBERATION

In the evening of August 24, Captain Dronne, sent by Leclerc as an advance guard, slalomed between the German defenses and ended up in the Place de l'Hôtel-de-Ville with three tanks crewed by Spanish Republicans. The electricity supply was immediately reinstated on the orders of the Resistance, and the city's church bells rang out full peal for many long minutes.

No one who lived through those days lived in vain.

In Bourg-la-Reine we met our first liberators in the late afternoon. That they were French seemed like a generous gift from the gods. Gallois-Cocteau, a tough man if ever there was one, was quite unable to speak and could not see for tears when Leclerc first appeared, and had muttered: "My boy, my boy, no emotion, we have serious work to do." We had lumps in our throats as we contemplated those three tank drivers, who smiled at our show of feeling. (But I could not quite banish a shameful sense of disappointment. I had become so used to the boots and tailored uniforms of the Germans that I found their mechanics' overalls distinctly unmilitary, with the front pockets so full it made them look like portly lawyers.) Then their internal radios crackled and the tank commander advised us calmly to move away a little. Ten seconds later he opened fire on a German armored car that loomed up in front of us. It managed to get away, leaving a trail of blood.

A more banal father would have kept his children indoors. Ours took us out at dawn the next day, onto the *route nationale*. He knew that this was going to be a day worth living, even if it were the last. A ragtag army was slowly making its way towards Paris cheered on by ecstatic crowds lining the route. We marched, with many others, alongside Leclerc's tanks and the Maquisard lorries from the Loiret, which were also coming to the rescue. The column halted frequently. Women took advantage to pull themselves up onto the tanks, proffering their mouths and their bodies, in an admirable gesture of patriotism. I suddenly felt a military vocation coming on. Sporadic gunfire crackled, scattering us like sparrows. The lipstick-streaked soldiers leaped down and fired back at random. We did not give a damn. Death seemed inconceivable. I could not remember ever having felt so happy. At the Porte d'Orléans, where there had been some quite serious fighting, I lost the rest of my family in the crowd, but felt no fear: Paris would look after me. On the way back to the house in the Avenue de l'Observatoire, I saw a mob in the Rue du Val-de-Grâce. A man was thrown from a fourth-floor window and smashed onto the pavement. He was an Indo-Chinese student, well known in the neighborhood. The crowd was yelling: "Death to the Japanese." A dozen Indo-Chinese met their deaths in this way. They were hard times for all that.

Because the avenue was being sprayed by German gunfire, my father had fixed up a ladder from the Rue Herschel. I climbed in through the window as my parents had done, and, overwhelmed by the sense of history, I began to write a diary, which was to be abandoned three days later. Outside, Fabien's men, with the help of Leclerc's tanks, were fighting the 700 Germans dug in at the Jardin du Luxembourg, with their Panther tanks. The final outcome was never in doubt, but the neighborhood lived in fear of all those tons of explosives stockpiled under the Senate: would not the men of the Luftwaffe, confirmed Nazis, choose to die beneath the ruins, taking us all with them, rather than surrender? The German strongholds fell one after another, but the Luxembourg could not be taken. Even tanks failed to knock out the blockhouses whose embrasures were at ground level, and difficult to get at. Fabien succeeded in the end by a stroke of genius. He reversed trucks filled with sand and tipped them all down onto the embrasures, rendering them sightless. The German defense was disabled. And at six in the evening we were allowed out.

At the top of the avenue, by the entrance to the Jardin du Luxembourg, the little German blockhouse stood disemboweled. Unlike the others, it was a pillbox just high enough to take a man, but the bullets of the Maquisards had kept ricocheting off the concrete. A tank had been needed. I can still hear the sound of its single shell. It had decapitated the German inside. Someone examining the lock observed that his superiors had double-locked him inside his concrete coffin. My military calling weakened. The smell of burnt flesh was surprisingly strong. People spat on his corpse. Ten meters away among the shattered fragments of the gates of the Jardin du Luxembourg, I noticed a glaucous slug; it was his eyeball.

Further inside the gardens, where people now play *boules*, they exhumed the tortured bodies, their eyes put out, of seven Frenchmen killed on August 19.

That night, Paris smelled of death and gunpowder.

Four years and 46 days had gone by since the Wehrmacht had entered the city.

The following day we watched the parade from the Arc de Triomphe to Notre-Dame. Our joy was supreme. After having listened for so long and so religiously to General de Gaulle, we finally saw him with our own eyes. He was even taller than we had imagined. The prophecy of Brossolette was coming true—Brossolette who had sacrificed himself so that it might one day come true—"De Gaulle, on the poignant day of victory, will be carried aloft the length of the Champs-Élysées, on a wave of our womens' tears of joy, to ceaseless bursts of cheering." He had not however predicted the dangerous bursts of gunfire from mysterious rooftop gunmen, which, while not intending to kill, flattened the crowds like a storm in a cornfield. I was drunk with emotion, drowning in happiness. And with good reason; subsequently reading the inevitable tale of naked ambition and infighting that was already going on, I know that history has put aside these vicissitudes, and will always remember August 26, 1944, as the day that pure emotion transported the city.

Night fell and I went off wandering. I took a walk along the banks of the Seine under the Tuileries where Leclerc's troops were bivouacked, and heard a strange refrain. The melody was interwoven with a profusion of long sighs, brief moanings, and stifled cries. It took me a little while to understand that hundreds of men and women were up there in bed together. Transfixed—God forgive me—with near-religious feeling, I spent a long moment there listening to Paris make love.

Paris becomes German

Paris in Mourning

After eight months of intermittent "phoney war" on various distant fronts, Paris woke on May 10, 1940, to rather ominous news: At 5:35 AM the Germans had implemented their "Plan Yellow" and were invading Belgium, Luxembourg, and the Netherlands. The unthinkable followed on May 13, when German Panzers crossed the Meuse at Dinant, Monthermé, and Sedan, penetrated the French line, and swept around the rear of the defensive armies deployed in Belgium. As the crisis deepened, the government of the one, indivisible secular Republic, led by Premier Paul Reynaud and War Minister Édouard Daladier, went in solemn procession to Notre-Dame on May 19 to pray before the sacred relics of Saint Geneviève and Saint Louis for the salvation of France. After driving the British into the sea at Dunkirk, the Wehrmacht plunged beyond the Somme on June 5, while the Luftwaffe, which had commanded the air from the very start, bombed Paris on June 3, albeit without subjecting it to the fire storm already meted out to Rotterdam. On June 13, French engineers destroyed the city's petrol reserves stored in the suburbs, covering the city in a mourning veil of smoke and soot.

1

1. *The Champs-Élysées on May 10, 1940.*

2. *The results of enemy bombing.*

3. *Burning gasoline stocks at Levallois-Perret, June 12, 1940.*

4. *Premier Paul Reynaud, Labor Minister Charles Pomaret, and Armaments Minister Raoul Dautry inspecting a bomb crater.*

3

The Germans Arrive

"They're coming!" With this terrified cry, Parisians fled their homes en masse, the social and political consequences of which would be dire. The great Exodus began on May 15 in a flood of refugees from Belgium and northern France. It gathered force as Parisians too began to stream out of the city, especially after the air raids of June 3. But once the government and the ministries slipped away during the night of June 9–10, a general panic set in, fueled by fear of bombs, Huns, or almost anything. Between June 10 and June 13 the trains were mobbed and the roads to the Loire Valley clogged with hundreds of thousands of people rushing southward by foot, bicycle, and automobile. By June 14 the French capital had lost all but some 700,000 of its 2.8-million population. The emptiest quarters were the fashionable ones, whereas a third of the 14th arrondissement's working-class citizens had stayed put. On June 11 the new commander-in-chief, Weygand, informed Premier Reynaud and General Héring, commander of the "army of Paris," that the capital would be declared an open city. Paris, in brief, would be occupied without contest.

1. *The Exodus: Place de la Concorde around June 13, 1940.*

2. *Poster of June 11, 1940, declaring Paris an "open city."*

3. *Refugees from the Nord at the Porte de Clignancourt in early June 1940.*

60

Planes in the Place de la Concorde

The Occupier parades through
Paris. One German division took
command of the city, mainly as a precaution against any sudden military
reversal, but also for the sake of order. Remembering the turmoil that
came with the Prussians' siege of
Paris in 1870–71, the Germans prepared themselves for a collective outbreak of Parisian resentment, or at
least for individual acts of violence.
Nothing of the sort actually occurred,
other than a certain amount of sabotage in the suburbs. Thus, on June
18 a Fieseler-Storch reconnaissance
plane could land unimpeded in the
Place de la Concorde. Earlier, German forces had filed through the city
in an orderly and impeccable show of
victory. Paris, it seems, was well
worth a parade.

4. *A Fieseler-Storch in the Place de
la Concorde.*

5. *A German troop transport at Le
Bourget, June 1940.*

4

5

1

The Germans Move In

The Germans move in and take over. The Occupier requisitioned more and more housing for military organizations and soldiers on leave. Every branch of German service set up its quarters, either in public buildings (the Commandant of Paris at the Palais-Bourbon and the Luftwaffe in the Senate) or in hotels, such as the Prince de Galles on Avenue George-V. Homes were taken over for officers and their troops. Four large canteens or *Soldatenheim* came into being, one of them at the Café Wepler on Place Clichy. The Germans also commandeered restaurants, movie houses (with the Marignan, Paris, and Rex becoming *Soldatenkino*), and, of course, brothels. Parisians quipped that they had "lodgers on the German plan."

3

2

4

1. Soldatenheim *or military canteen,
Place Clichy.*

2. *The German Ambassador, Otto
Abetz, in conversation with General
von Stülpnagel, Commandant of
Paris, at the Hôtel Ritz.*

3. *The requisitioned Hôtel Prince de
Galles on Avenue George-V.*

4. *German newspapers for sale in the
Place de la Concorde.*

5. *Spectators at a military parade,
June 1940.*

On Their Best Behavior

The Germans are ever so correct. When the first of their units entered Paris, loudspeaker-equipped trucks broadcast an announcement: "Parisians! German troops will be passing through Paris for the next 48 hours. Stock what provisions you need, then go home and stay there. No demonstrations will be permitted...." The curfew was soon lifted, and when the citizenry ventured out again, they were more astonished than alarmed by their "correct" conquerors. Many seemed torn between shame and a kind of timorous relief. Simultaneously, the Nazis' propaganda machine set about to demonstrate—even if it meant falsifying the dates of photographs and newsreel clips—that the people of Paris had, from the very first, collaborated willingly and happily with their Occupying overlords. Dr. Goebbels unquestionably knew his business.

5

The Wehrmacht Takes Over

The Germans take command. The swastika flag first flew over the Arc de Triomphe on June 14, 1940. Until the end of the Occupation, the tricolore would thenceforth be banned in Paris as well as throughout northern France. The Nazi emblem hung from the façade of the Hôtel Meurice symbolized the conqueror's total power over the Parisian population, whose fate and daily existence lay in the hands of two high-ranking German officers. One of them, the *Militärbefehlshaber in Frankreich* (High Commandant of France), who reported directly to the chief commandant of the Western front, established a base in the Hôtel Majestic. His military and administrative authority extended over the entire Occupied Zone, except for three eastern *départements* and those of the Nord and the Pas-de-Calais. The post was held in succession by General Streccius, General Otto von Stülpnagel, and General Karl-Heinrich von Stülpnagel. Outside the *Militärbefehlshaber* stood the German Ambassador responsible for political affairs. Otto Abetz, seen on

the preceding page in conversation with General Otto von Stülpnagel, served in this capacity throughout most of the Occupation. The other important military officer was the Commandant of *Gross-Paris* (the capital as well as the Seine, Seine-et-Oise, and Seine-et-Marne), who had his headquarters at the Hôtel Meurice. For a long time General Schaumburg oversaw *Gross-Paris*, to be succeeded by General Dietrich von Choltitz, who remained in place until the end of the Occupation.

1. *Inspection by the* Feldgendarmerie.

2. *Place de l'Étoile.*

3. *Dinner at the Hôtel Meurice.*

4. *Dispatch riders outside the Hôtel Meurice.*

5. *Changing the guard at the Hôtel Meurice, headquarters of the German military government in Paris.*

3

4

5

Hitler in Paris

Hitler visits. At dawn on June 23, *der Führer* himself touched down at Le Bourget. First he went on a whirlwind tour of the Opéra before going back up the Champs-Élysées to the Trocadéro and the Eiffel Tower. Next came the Invalides, where he paused in meditation before Napoleon's Tomb. But neither the Sacré-Coeur, the Place des Vosges, nor the Sainte-Chapelle moved the great man, and by nine in the evening he had concluded his visit. On that same day Hitler remarked to Albert Speer, his favorite architect (later his Munitions Minister): "I have always dreamt of visiting Paris." A little later he added: "I've often wondered if Paris would have to be destroyed— but when we've finished our plans for Berlin, Paris will be no more than its shadow, so why destroy it?" How kind of *der Führer*!

1

1. *Hitler and his staff visiting Paris.*

2. *Hitler and General Keitel at Le Bourget, June 23, 1940.*

3. *After visiting the Eiffel Tower: Hitler with General Keitel, Albert Speer, confidential-secretary Martin Bormann, and media-relations chief Otto Dietrich.*

4. *Hitler posing before the Eiffel Tower.*

2

3

4

Revenge for Past Defeat

Hitler triumphs. While gracing the Tomb of Napoleon with his visit, the Führer could take satisfaction on other accounts. Three days earlier, for instance, the Germans had signed the Armistice, which ratified the utter defeat of their hereditary enemy and erased the humiliation of November 1918. France's civilian and military representatives had been taken to Rethondes for their rendezvous with Keitel in the same railroad car used for the German surrender at the end of World War I. What exquisite revenge! Moreover, the French officials had been given less than twenty-four hours in which to assimilate the nonnegotiable clauses of a veritable *Diktat*. By its terms, troops of the vanquished nation were to be disarmed, except for a 100,000-man force retained for purposes of internal order. The French state was also to pay a tribute by underwriting the cost of the Occupation. Meanwhile, French prisoners would not be released until a peace treaty could be signed; German political refugees must be surrendered; France was to be cut in two along a line running from Gex to the Spanish border by way of Chalon-sur-Saône, Moulins, and the outskirts of Tours and Angoulême, with a "free" zone on one side and an "occupied" zone, including Paris, on the other. On July 19, 1940, in a speech addressed to the new tenants of the Palais-Bourbon, Hitler extolled the superiority of German arms and took the opportunity to insult "that international arsonist" Churchill.

1. *Hitler on the steps of the Invalides following his visit to the Tomb of Napoleon.*

2. *After the rebroadcast of Hitler's speech at the Palais-Bourbon, the seat of France's Chamber of Deputies, on July 19, 1940.*

3. *The signing of the Franco-German armistice at Rethondes: left, General Huntziger, chief of the French delegation; right, General Keitel.*

1

2

3

The New Tourists

The Germans take tours. Early in the Occupation, the Wehrmacht organized cultural visits for soldiers on leave, usually including Versailles and a visit to the Louvre, where some galleries had been reopened even though the most important works remained in shelters or hidden away (a wise precaution, since Goering and certain other Nazi leaders took more than a connoisseur's interest in valuable works of art). Casts having replaced original statues on their pedestals, the new tourists had to view not the Venus de Milo but her understudy.

1. *German tourists at the Louvre.*

2. *Reopening of the Greek sculpture gallery at the Louvre, where General von Rundstedt and M. Merlin, the museum's Curator, admire the Venus de Milo.*

1

2

A Strange Tribute

The Germans pay homage. Whereas in Warsaw it had been strictly forbidden for the occupying forces to offer any mark of respect at monuments to the Polish dead, German soldiers on leave in Paris were required to render military honors to France's Tomb of the Unknown Soldier at the Arc de Triomphe. Nevertheless, it was in the vicinity of the Étoile that school children and college students, on November 11, 1940, made the first collective show of resistance against the Occupation.

3. *German troops at France's Tomb of the Unknown Soldier.*

4. *German troops viewing Rude's bas-relief entitled* La Marseillaise *on the Arc de Triomphe.*

3

4

German Boys and French Girls

The Germans become *flâneurs*, strolling through Paris. For the better part of a year, German soldiers felt safe in Paris, which appeared to welcome them like the tourists—rather particular ones, to be sure—that they very much wanted to be. Pictures from the spring of 1941 seem to reflect this mood of tranquility. Come summer of the same year, however, the first attacks on Wehrmacht personnel forced the authorities to impose rules of the strictest kind: no walking about alone, especially after dark, and no overly intimate relations with Frenchwomen. Indeed, German servicemen were reminded that they should not, in public, take the arm of "any female person."

1. *The Moulin-Rouge, June 1940.*

2. *Montmartre, June 1940.*

3. *Place du Tertre, 1941.*

4. *A German soldier at the Trocadéro opposite the Eiffel Tower.*

1

2

3

73

4

Plundering the Shops

In their methodical way, the Germans exploited conquered France by three economic devices: the tribute, the clearing agreement, and an artificial rate of exchange for the Reichsmark. As a result, France had to subvene the cost of the Occupation, which ran to 400 million francs a day from June 1940 to May 1941, 300 million from May 1941 to November 1942, and 500 million after the Occupation included the former Free Zone south of Moulins. Under the "compensation agreement" of November 14, 1940, the Banque de France had to finance the continuing imbalance of trade between itself and the Reich, since Germany exported almost nothing to France. In addition, the Reichsmark had been deliberately overvalued at twice its

1

2
3

market worth, which endowed the Occupation troops with an excess of purchasing power. To sustain this inequity, the Germans insisted that French prices be controlled at unrealistically low levels. Thus, whereas earlier German invaders had looted, the new Wehrmacht—officers and noncoms alike—simply bought cheaply whatever they fancied, thereby becoming connoisseurs of wines, brandies, and fine lingerie, all of which disappeared across the Rhine.

1. *Baggage of German soldiers on leave (a photograph suppressed by the German censors on October 6, 1940).*

2, 3, 4, 5, 6. *Germans admiring the quality of French merchandise.*

4

5

6

To the Victor Go the Spoils

For the Reich, France constituted the champion milch-cow of Occupied Europe, increasingly exploited for the benefit of the German war machine, which pre-empted a fifth of the country's agricultural production and a good part of its livestock, particularly the horses. As raw materials became scarcer, orders went out to melt down a number of statues in Paris for their content of nonferrous metals. Neither Victor Hugo nor Sergeant Bobillot, a hero of the Tonkin campaigns, escaped the crucible. Along with the official procurement system came a network of clandestine purchasing offices, with its own warehouses and docks, operating under commercial cover and effective political protection. These enterprises were known as the "Otto offices," after an agent of the *Abwehr* (the German counter-intelligence service) who had opened the first of them in Paris. In the twenty months of their activity, they bought a wide array of merchandise for an estimated 50 million francs. (As a general rule, such wartime sums must be multiplied by 60 to obtain an approximate equivalent in *old* francs.) For efficiency's sake, the Germans recruited French touts and go-betweens who became monarchs of the black market, working hand-in-glove with the Occupier. A certain M. Joseph, alias Joanovici, a onetime scrap-iron dealer, is said to have done 4 billion francs' worth of business. For some, therefore, Collaboration was to be toasted in champagne.

1. *Requisitioned horses.*

2. *A large German warehouse.*

Off to the Races

The Society for the Improvement of Bloodstock knew how to plead its cause. As a consequence, the racetracks at Auteuil and Vincennes reopened on October 12, 1940. At stake, according to the argument, was the survival of French breeders, not to mention the dissatisfaction of pari-mutuel bettors, a fact noted by the German authorities. In 1941, it was once again possible to attend the races at Maisons-Laffitte and Longchamp, although getting there could be haphazard. In 1943, there may have been fewer meetings than in 1938, but almost as many people passed through the turnstiles. Of course, the sport had found a new following.

3, 4, 5. *Auteuil.*

3

4

5

Bon Appétit

The average Parisian lunched and dined at restaurants classified A to D and offering meals at 10 to 35 francs. Here, no one risked indigestion from overindulgence. But for those with enough money—indeed a lot of it—there were other establishments where, beginning at 1,000 francs a person, one could eat well and drink the finest wines. And so it was at Bagatelle or at L'Aiglon on the Rue de Berri, which billed itself as a place in which one could be served "in an atmosphere of charm and elegance." At Fouquet's, Chapon Fin, Pré Catalan, Drouant, Prunier, and the like, well-healed gluttons might still enjoy themselves, selecting from menus considerately presented in French and German. The *beau monde* never suffered a shortage of butter.

1. *L'Aiglon on the Rue de Berri, 1940. Among the diners are Fernand Gravey, Jacqueline Delubac, the painter Kees Van Dongen, Danielle Darrieux, and André Luguet.*

2, 3. *L'Aiglon, 1940.*

4

5

7

6

Paris by Night

*P**aris bie Nacht*, the city's accustomed nightlife, was in full swing again within a week of the Wehrmacht's arrival. The German authorities proved quite liberal in regard to nightclubs and cabarets, whatever their specialty, singing or striptease. The *Pariser Zeitung* published a map showing hundreds of well-established places where boredom could be escaped. Half of them (the Grand Jeu and the Tabarin, for instance) were in Montmartre and the rest about equally divided between the Champs-Élysées and Montparnasse. With the Teutonic warriors evincing a marked preference for girlie shows, the Moulin de la Galette was able to keep *La Bière et le Nu* running almost permanently.

4. *The Moulin de la Galette in 1940.*

5. *The Grand Jeu.*

6. *The Cabaret Mimi Pinson in 1940.*

7. *The Moulin de la Galette.*

An der Musik

The Germans, as everyone knows, have a passion for music. And with music their propagandists hoped to foster goodwill. The hundredth anniversary of *The Flying Dutchman* and the hundred-fiftieth anniversary of the death of Mozart brought appearances in Paris by such distinguished conductors and soloists as Willem Mengelberg and Wilhelm Kempff. The young Herbert von Karajan also made his debut in the French capital about this time. The Berlin Philharmonic played at the Palais de Chaillot on July 17, 1944. Concert halls and the Opéra were full and music-lovers happy. Nor did Parisians with less money and less well-developed taste find themselves neglected. Every Sunday the Place de l'Opéra, the parvis of Notre-Dame, and the Jardin des Tuileries played host to military bands performing medleys of marches, folk songs, and excerpts from Wagner and Richard Strauss. In November 1941, 300 musicians from every branch of the Wehrmacht gave a concert at the Palais de Chaillot, under the baton of a "helmeted conductor."

1. *A public concert.*

2, 3. *Audiences for the Germans' free concerts, 1940.*

A One-Ring Circus

The war and its deprivations brought much hardship to the circus, causing Pinder and the Amar brothers to remain closed. Bouglione, Médrano, and Jean Houcke at the Grand Palais supplemented their bills with music-hall numbers, pantomime (*Snow White* and *Ali Baba*), or demonstrations by, of all people, the Olympic athlete Ladoumègue. Crowds flocked to the Médrano to watch the horsemanship of Michaela Busch, daughter of a rider in Berlin's Grand Circus. The audience included not only children but also German circus buffs, like the Wehrmacht officer who, on Friday November 13, 1940, drove off Royal, a tiger on the verge of mauling the movie star Gina Manès, who had rashly tried her hand as a tamer in the big-cat cage.

4. *German soldiers and nurses from the Occupier's Army Medical Corps.*

5. *Busch horses at the Cirque Médrano.*

DEUTSCHLAND SIEGT AN ALLEN FRONTEN

LA NOUVELLE EUROPE SE FERA DONT SERONT EXCLUES L'ANGLETERRE ET LA RUSSIE. ON CHASSERA L'ANGLETERRE DANS LES OCÉANS ET LA RUSSIE TARTARE DANS LES STEPPES.
VICTOR HUGO

A New Order in Europe

The Occupation and its open partisans strove to convince the French people that France, if she collaborated whole-heartedly, would enjoy a favored position in "the new Europe." Two exhibitions at the Grand Palais, inaugurated with great ceremony in May 1941 and April 1942 by dignitaries from both Germany and Vichy, set out to prove the point with a lavish display of oversized maps, scale models of farms and dams, two continuous movie programs, a 1,400-seat theater—and copious refreshments. Pride of place went to the historical figures deemed the great forebears of a united Europe: Charlemagne, Napoleon, and Victor Hugo, not to mention Joan of Arc, burned at the stake by you-know-whom. In glorious conclusion came a eulogy to the "New Life" (the actual title of the 1942 exhibition), as already lived in the Reich, whose benevolently protective forces were winning on all fronts, if one could believe the legend along the façade of the Chamber of Deputies crowned by a giant "V" for Victory.

4

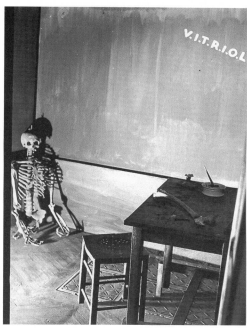

V.I.T.R.I.O.L

5

6

REP∴MAC∴

L'AVEU !

La maçonnerie reconnait par les dates inscrites sur cette statue, qu'elle est responsable :

DE LA RÉVOLUTION BOURGEOISE DE 1789

DE LA RÉVOLUTION ÉMEUTIÈRE DE 1848

ET DE LA COMMUNE DE 1870.

The Red Peril

After the German invasion of Russia in June 1941, the New Europe fought toe-to-toe with the hydra-headed monster of Communism. As part of the campaign, an exhibition entitled "Bolshevism Against Europe" opened in April 1942 at the Salle Wagram. No admission was charged, and school teachers were strongly urged to take their classes. Even greater *succès d'estime* awaited an exhibition dealing with another enemy of the "New Europeans." This was "Freemasonry Unveiled," which in October–November 1940 held sway at the Petit Palais, where visitors could see furniture, robes, and regalia confiscated from Masonic lodges. The show included the sensational feature of a skeleton in the "meditation closet" to which apprentices must retire before their initiation. To drive the point home, a "Directory of Lodge Brothers" was on sale. For the many with paranoid fears about "secret societies," a visit to the exhibition seemed well worth the effort.

1. *"V" for Victory at the Chamber of Deputies, above a banner reading "Germany Victorious on All Fronts!"*

2. *Propaganda posters bearing the likeness of Victor Hugo above a quotation from the great man: "There shall be a new Europe, from which England and Russia shall be shut out; we shall chase the English into the sea and the Tatar Russians back to their steppes."*

3. *The fashion stand at the "European France" exhibition.*

4, 5, 6. *Exhibits at the "Freemasonry Unveiled" show.*

Strangle the Press

The Militärbefehlshaber service included a propaganda wing, which immediately went to work on the Paris press. The *Propaganda Abteilung* established its own information agency, rationed newsprint, oversaw distribution, and, through the "Groupe Hibbelen," purchased outright half the capital's printed media. After the arrival of the Wehrmacht, German censors began examining galley proofs, and to nip editorial resistance in the bud, the Propaganda Abteilung provided editors with regular instructions, every day for political and military news and thrice weekly for economic news. A small number of papers—for instance, *Toute la Vie*, a weekly established in 1941 for the purpose of glorifying the National Revolution—stayed somewhat outside the German orbit, whereas *L'Oeuvre* (a daily taken over by Marcel Déat and his neo-socialists) or *Le Petit Parisien* (a mass-circulation daily with a press run of half a million, even in 1942, and a journalistic tie-in with Doriot's group and the reporters of the Collaborationist weekly *Je Suis Partout*) was unequivocally on the New European side. The chairman of the "Press Corporation" was Jean Luchaire, who once supported Aristide Briand, the French statesman long in favor of genuine cooperation between France and Germany, and now published *Les Nouveaux Temps*, a daily whose survival depended on continuing subsidies from Abetz. A major presence in *le Tout-Paris*, Luchaire was a valued dinner guest who may be seen in plate 2 addressing an exclusive audience that included, on his right, Schleier, Otto Abetz' deputy, and, on his left, Rahn, counselor at the German Embassy.

1. *Kiosk at the Étoile.*
2. *The "Press Banquet."*

The Jew in France

Jews, from time immemorial, may have been regarded as the sworn enemies of Europe, but it was not until September 5, 1941, that "The Jew and France" exhibition opened at the Palais Berlitz. The delay reflected a determination, on the part of the organizers and their French as well as German "scientific experts," to do things properly. Official anti-Semitism, predictably, characterized Jews as phagocytes permeating every aspect of the nation's political, economic, and cultural life. Unequivocally, they were declared to control 95 percent of the banking system, 70 percent of the press, and 40 percent of the fashion industry. Slath-ered over it all was an age-old primitive or popular anti-Semitism drawn directly from the delusions of the Nazis, who held it a civic duty to learn how to detect Jews by their "hooked noses," "protruding ears," and "furtive glances." Even the hoariest of libels were trotted out, including allegations of the ritual murder of non-Jewish children, the pretext for some of the most appalling pogroms in history.

3. *The Palais Berlitz in September 1941.*

4. *A statue at the entrance to the Jewish exhibition in September 1941.*

The Radio Gets Through

France, a country with some 5.3 million radios in 1943, became the battlefield for a "war of the wavelengths," and, beginning in 1941, the Vichy government spared nothing in its effort to expand the audience for the "National Radio Network" as a foil to the BBC's French-language broadcasts. For the photograph in plate 3, Propaganda Abteilung posed a group of "listeners" supposedly enthralled by the broadcast that Admiral Darlan made on May 23, 1941. In the spring of 1943 the French government shifted all radio services to Paris, mainly for the sake of limiting the influence of Radio-Paris itself. The new Paris facility, made up of five prewar stations and equipped with a high-powered transmitter, functioned entirely under German control. Indeed, its director was Bofinger, formerly director of Radio-Stuttgart. Fifteen broadcast hours devoted to songs, variety shows, and classical concerts sugar-coated the pill of seven (later ten) daily newscasts.

1. The English bookstore W. H. Smith on the Rue de Rivoli transformed into a German bookstore in 1941.

2. "The New France," November 26, 1941.

3. "Listeners" during Admiral Darlan's address to his countrymen, May 23, 1941.

1

2

3

Paris
collaborates

1

2

Pétain Leads the Collaboration

The armistice signed by the French at Rethondes on June 22, 1940, imposed draconian conditions on their conquered nation, including a request that all officials in the Northern Zone "collaborate with [the German military authorities] in a full and proper manner." Given the continued resistance of Great Britain, Hitler determined against a peace treaty in the West, whereupon Philippe Pétain chose political collaboration as the best course for France. He communicated this decision to Hitler when the two met on October 24, 1940, at Montoire, a small town in the Vendôme, after which the Third Reich and the French State entered into official Collaboration with one another. For Hitler, however, Collaboration did not mean partnership; rather, state Collaboration became a "lemon-squeeze" that provided a field day for the cartoonists of the underground newspaper *Combat*. Not surprisingly, Pétainists became ever-more scarce with the passage of time, although in the Occupied Zone, where the *Marseillaise* and the tricolore were banned, a certain pro-Pétain sentiment persisted, still discernible as late as April 26, 1944, when the Marshal visited Paris for a service memorializing bomb victims.

Kollaborer, c'est être roulé.

DONNANT, DONNANT.

Hitler : - *Donne-moi la montre, je te donnerai l'heure.*

1. *Marshal Pétain's car passing through the Place du Châtelet, April 26, 1944.*

2. *Marshal Pétain meeting with Hitler, accompanied by von Ribbentrop, in Hitler's private railway car, at Montoire station, October 24, 1940.*

3. *A* Combat *cartoon satirizing the Collaboration.*

4. *The opening, on May 30, 1942, of the "New Europe" exhibition at the Grand Palais, attended by (from left to right) General von Barkhausen, General von Stülpnagel, Ambassador Fernand de Brinon, and the dark-mustached Pierre Laval.*

89

Ashes for Coal

Pierre Laval, an isolated veteran of France's political wars, began life in the early years of the century as a militant Pacifist and Socialist. By the 1930s, however, he had become an adversary of the Popular Front and a proponent of appeasement towards Fascist Italy and Nazi Germany. Soon after the Occupation began, Laval emerged as the arch symbol of Collaboration. At first he moved too rapidly and, on December 13, 1940, got himself dismissed from the government, only to be spirited into Paris by Germany's Ambassador, Otto Abetz. In his official place stepped Admiral Darlan, the stubborn protector of France's unconquered navy who finally agreed to cooperate with the Third Reich out of rabid Anglophobia. However, Hitler, by his own duplicity, rather spoiled this opportunity, with the result that he had to accept the reappointment of Laval to the Ministry of Foreign Affairs on April 18, 1942. Laval thought it still possible to collaborate, but in practice he could do no more than camouflage a bad situation, especially after November 1942, when Vichy lost the last vestige of its bargaining power. Beginning in December 1940, Vichy simply maintained a kind of Ambassador in Paris, an appointment held by the zealous Collaborationist Fernand de Brinon, a long-standing member of the Comité France-Allemagne. And so, on December 15, 1940, when Hitler made the symbolic gesture of having the ashes of "L'Aiglon" sent from Vienna to rest beside the tomb of his father, Napoleon I, at the Invalides—a hundred years, to the day, after the Emperor's own remains had been placed there—a good many Parisians exclaimed: "They take our coal and send us back ashes!"

1. *General von Stülpnagel, accompanied by Colonel Speidel, meet with General Bridoux and Ambassador Fernand de Brinon.*

2. *Admiral Darlan.*

3. *Pierre Laval.*

4, 5, 6. *Ceremonial "Return of the Ashes" to the Invalides.*

Books Better Burned

The Occupier took every measure to win at psychological warfare. Among the weapons used were the daily newspapers *Pariser Zeitung* and *Signal*, both bimonthly color photo-magazines that consisted of little more than translated articles originally written for a German readership. The German Institute in France, headed by Karl Epting, proved more adaptable to the local scene, offering courses in German and a series of lectures, some by persons of distinction, delivered in French to a select audience. When the Rive Gauche bookstore opened on April 25, 1941, at the corner of Boulevard Saint-Michel and Place de la Sorbonne, it became "France's outlet for German books," an enterprise managed by Henri Bardèche and a board composed of three Germans and three Frenchmen. Here it was that Lucien Rebatet, a competent musicologist and critic on the staff of *Je Suis Partout*, signed copies of *Les Décombres*, a massive, autobiographical work in which the notorious anti-Semitic, Fascist author settled accounts with Maurras, the right wing, the clergy, and the generals. *Les Décombres* became *the* event of 1942, at least within the narrow confines of Collaborationist Paris. Also active in this small world was Dr. Destouches, who as the pseudonymous Louis-Ferdinand Céline, could be found attending conferences at the Institute for Jewish Questions. After coming to the fore in 1932 with the publication of his novel *Voyage au bout de la nuit*, Céline went on to issue such anti-Semitic diatribes as *Bagatelles pour un massacre*.

1. *Louis-Ferdinand Céline (center) and Louis Lambert attending a conference at the Institute for Jewish Questions, May 1941.*

2. *The Rive Gauche bookstore.*

3. *Lucien Rebatet signing copies of* Les Décombres *at the Rive Gauche bookstore, 1942.*

4. Signal's *display window on the Avenue des Champs-Élysées, December 1942–January 1943.*

2

3

4

Cultural Exchange

The Occupier arranged free trips to Germany for French actors, pianists, and painters, who found, certainly, a warm, if not entirely disinterested, welcome beyond the Rhine. The most successful propaganda gesture was the invitation that French intellectuals received to attend the Congress of European Writers held at Weimar on November 21–26, 1942, as part of "the week of the German war book." On their return, at the Gare de l'Est, Gerhard Heller, "special attaché" to the cultural service of the German Embassy, was photographed with two leaders of France's Collaborationist intelligentsia: Drieu La Rochelle and Robert Brasillach. La Rochelle, author of *Gilles* and owner of *La Nouvelle Revue Française*, would commit suicide in Paris in March 1945. Meanwhile, Brasillach, managing editor of *Je Suis Partout* until the summer of 1943, gave himself up after the arrest of his mother. Condemned to death, he was executed by firing squad on February 6, 1945.

1. *A delegation of French artists leaving for Germany.*

2. *Robert Brasillach in the dock, hearing himself sentenced to die.*

3. *French writers returning from Germany, November 1941: (left to right) Lieutenant Gerhard Heller, Drieu La Rochelle, Georg Rabuse (second row), Robert Brasillach, Abel Bonnard, André Fraigneau, and Karl Heinz Bremer, aide to Karl Epting at the German Institute in Paris.*

2

3

1

A Brilliant Ambassador

Otto Abetz, "German Ambassador to the Military Commandant" in France, had belonged to the Comité France-Allemagne before the Nazis came to power. He remained with the society after 1933 and even won the confidence of von Ribbentrop. While advocating a policy of unwavering firmness towards conquered France, Abetz also advised against reducing her to total subservience. Moreover, he sought to endow Collaboration with a certain cachet, especially since, having once studied art, he regarded himself as a man of culture. Here, in plate 2, he can be seen with his wife on May 26, 1941, leaving the Parisian house where Richard Wagner composed *The Flying Dutchman*. Even the more austere Otto von Stülpnagel, Supreme Military Commandant in France, saw fit to lend his presence to a reception given at the Paris Opéra in honor of a visiting troupe from the Berlin Opera, an occasion that drew both German and French VIPs. Collaboration, of course, meant more than politics or the arts; it also entailed commerce, though less overtly. On January 11, 1941, a banquet at the Royal-Monceau was attended by General von Barkhausen, the French "technocrats" Barnaud, Pucheu, and Bichelonne, as well as by thirty-five representatives of banking, industry, and commerce, a group whose aggregate worth counted in the billions of francs.

1. *General von Barkhausen at the "Treason Dinner," January 11, 1941.*

2. *Ambassador and Mrs. Otto Abetz in 1941 visiting an exhibition devoted to Richard Wagner in the house where the composer wrote* The Flying Dutchman.

3. *General von Stülpnagel attending a dinner at the Paris Opéra in honor of a visiting troupe from the Berlin Opera.*

2

3

Propaganda

The first task of the German propagandists was to purge French publishing. (An "Otto" list, prohibiting the sale of certain books, appeared as early as September 1940.) Next, they undertook to censor books before publication. Simultaneously, the Germans wanted to promote their culture, an objective pursued, for example, by the writer Ernst Jünger, whose later *Diary* is a rather self-serving account of the period. Heinrich George, who appeared in a February 1941 performance of Schiller's *Kabale und Liebe* in Paris, was guest of honor at a reception given by Abetz. There, he received the congratulations of the well-known French actor Harry Baur, who had just finished his movie *La Symphonie d'une vie*, made on location in Austria. Le Tout-Paris that Collaborated, or maintained social relations, with the Occupier flocked to an exhibition of work by Arno Breker, whose "Olympia of heroes and giants" had made him a favorite of the Führer. The show was opened at the Orangerie with much ceremony on May 15, 1942, by Abel Bonnard, a member of the Académie Française and a minister in the Vichy government. Among the thronging guests could be found van Dongen, Derain, Dunoyer de Segonzac, Serge Lifar, and Benoist-Méchin. Even the aged Maillol bestirred himself to attend, as did Sacha Guitry.

1. *The Arno Breker exhibition.*

2. *Arno Breker, official sculptor of the Third Reich.*

3. *A few days before he was arrested and tortured by the Gestapo, Harry Baur with the German actor Heinrich George.*

4. *During a reception at the German Embassy in Paris honoring the Schiller Theater, February 1941, Ambassador Otto Abetz and Consul-General Schleier congratulate the actor Heinrich George.*

5. *Paul Wegener in the Schiller Theater's performance of* Kabale und Liebe *at the Comédie Française, March 1, 1941.*

6. *The German writer Ernst Jünger.*

99

1

French Fascists: The PPF

The Fall of France cleared the way for a number of hitherto marginal politicians, who, after a short spell in Vichy, where they found less welcome than they expected, returned to Paris. In the Occupied capital they could abuse the Vichy "reactionaries" to their hearts' content, while also declaring themselves "revolutionaries," French to be sure but even more so "European," and advocating Franco-German cooperation at all levels, even military. In short, they became Collaborationists. Some of them had been extreme right-wing activists between the wars, like the Great War veteran Marcel Bucard who in 1933 founded *francisme*, a Fascist-inspired group seen parading their banners in plate 4. In 1936 Jacques Doriot, a powerful speaker and the onetime white-haired boy of the Comintern, had founded another Fascist group, the Parti Populaire Français, or PPF, after his expulsion from the French Communist Party. From 1941 on, Doriot was wholly committed to the Germans. The Rassemblement National Populaire or RNP was a new party, the brainchild of Marcel Déat, a teacher and former Socialist who had converted to ideological Fascism. The RNP and the militant PPF quarreled endlessly. Divided among themselves, bereft of popular support, and repudiated by the vast majority of Frenchmen, the Collaborationists quickly became dependent on (financially and otherwise) and indeed the captives of their German sponsors.

2

3

1. *Posters for the Rassemblement National Populaire, February 1941.*

2. *Jacques Doriot speaking to the PPF Congress at the Salle Wagram, November 11, 1942.*

3. *Demonstration following the PPF Congress at the Salle Wagram.*

4. *Marcel Bucard arriving at the Vélodrome d'Hiver, July 3, 1943.*

4

HONNEUR
HEROISME
ESPRIT DE SACRIFICE

101

The French Militia

On January 30, 1944, Vichy organized the French Militia "for public service" in the Unoccupied, or Free, Zone. It comprised both auxiliaries, male and female, who retained their full-time jobs, and the Francs-Gardes, who lived in barracks and trained to keep public order. By the end of January 1944 the Germans agreed to allow the Militia to function in the Occupied Zone as well. Some weeks earlier, the organization's secretary-general, Joseph Darnand, a veteran commando formerly involved with such right-wing groups as Action Française and the Cagoulards, had agreed that he and his immediate staff should be integrated with the Waffen-SS, thereby making an irreversible commitment to Collaboration. In plate 3, "Jo" Darnand, wearing his Militia uniform, can be seen chatting with General Oberg, "Supreme Commander of the SS and the police in France." In 1944 the SS systematically exploited the Militia as auxiliaries to fight the Resistance (for example on the Glières plateau in the Haute-Savoie) as well as to track down saboteurs and foreign Jews. After the Allies landed, it was the Militia, in both northern and southern zones, that perpetrated the worst atrocities.

1. *Posters, 1944.*

2. *March 1944: a Francs-Gardes billet in the former synagogue in Auteuil.*

3. *French Militia taking the oath in the Invalides courtyard, July 1, 1944: (left to right) de Brinon, Hagen (Oberg's aide, second row), Oberg, the Gestapo or SS chief in France from 1942 through 1944, Darnand (in profile), and SS Colonel Helmut Knochen.*

4. *Young men signing up at Militia headquarters.*

3

4

SI TU VEUX QUE LA FRANCE VIVE
TU COMBATTRAS DANS LA WAFFEN
CONTRE LE BOLCHEVISME

Henriot the Traitor

In 1944, Frenchmen came to realize that the Militia was taking charge in an increasingly authoritarian police state. Darnand, by his appointment on December 30, 1943, as Secretary-General for the Maintenance of Order, had gained effective control of the internal security forces, the prisons, and the radio. His creature, Philippe Henriot, the State Secretary for Information and Propaganda, delivered twice-daily commentaries on the national radio network—and not entirely without success. Since June 1941—and before he was assassinated in Paris on June 28, 1944, by an independent unit of the Resistance—Henriot had believed the Christian West, whose secular arm he saw as Adolph Hitler, to be engaged in a death struggle against the "Bolshevik Anti-Christ."

Yet, despite his eloquence, the Militia was detested by almost all Frenchmen and Frenchwomen. Even the emblem selected by Henriot for the Militia—the zodiacal "gamma" symbolizing the steadfast ram and spring renewal—served the Resistance, which transformed it into the initial letter of the word *Vendu* or "Sold" (as in "down the river"). With this, the Militia appeared all the more to be the Occupier's henchmen who waged civil war against their own countrymen.

1. *Christmas dinner for children of the Waffen-SS, December 30, 1942, at the Cercle Aryen, 5 Boulevard Montmartre.*

2. *German propaganda poster.*

The
show goes on

1

LE PRÉSIDENT KRÜGER

2

3

Movies as Propaganda

Since Leni Riefenstahl's documentary film on the 1936 Olympics, held at Nüremberg, it had been evident that the Nazis regarded the cinema as an effective instrument of propaganda. However, German movies released in Paris during the Occupation constituted a mixed bag, ranging from musical comedies (*Cora Terry*, for example, starring the dancer Marika Rökk) and operettas laid in Vienna or Paris, such as Willi Forst's *Bel Ami*, to spectaculars on the order of *The Fantastic Adventures of Baron Münchhausen*, a color feature that took ten months to make for Josef von Baky and earned great admiration for its breakthrough in special effects. But the cinema also proved subservient to the political objectives of the Third Reich by attacking the enemies of the Master Race. Hans Steinhoff, whose *Hitler Youth* Paris saw in 1942, threw mud at England in his *President Krüger*, a film with a cast of 40,000 that used the Boer War as a text for inveighing against the supposed baseness, egotism, and hypocrisy of the English.

1. *German newsreel.*

2. *Hans Steinhoff's* President Krüger, *with Emil Jannings.*

3. *Gustav Ucicky's* The Postmaster, *with Heinrich George.*

4. Bel Ami *at the Imperiale.*

5. *A German movie poster scrawled over with graffiti: "Boche film: don't go."*

6. *Carl Froehlich's* Pages immortelles, *with Marika Rökk.*

4

5

Zarah LEANDER   Marika RÖKK
PAGES IMMORTELLES
Un Film de CARL FRŒLICH de la U. F. A.
avec HANS STÜWE, ARIBERT WÄSCHER, LÉO SLEZAK
Musique de PETER TCHAÏKOWSKY

6

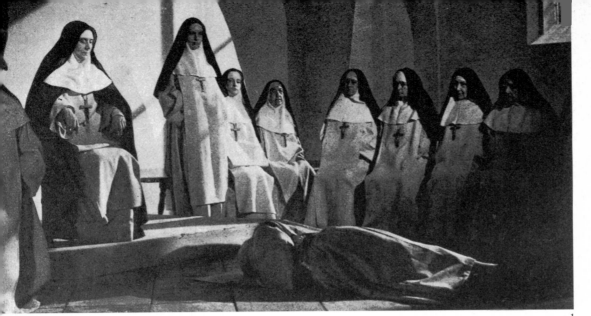

1

2

The Stars Still Glow

The movie houses remained filled throughout the Occupation, and Parisians could always count on a program complete with newsreel, documentary, and feature film. To be sure, the Propaganda Abteiling kept close watch on everything relating to the cinema. Not only did it license newsreels; it also banned all films released after October 1, 1937. In May 1941 the Germans prohibited American and British films entirely. Censors reviewed full-length features as soon as they were shot, thereby encouraging producers to censor themselves. Continental, a subsidiary of the German UFA studios, bought into production companies, acquired theater chains, and released thirty films in France. Goebbels had declared that the French should watch movies that were "light, trivial, and, if possible, stupid"—epithets scarcely applicable to Robert Bresson's first full-length feature, *Les Anges du péché*, made in 1943 with the screenplay by Jean Giraudoux. Nor could they be used to describe Jean Delannoy's *L'Éternal Retour*, a modern version of Tristan and Yseult written by Jean Cocteau and played by Madeleine Sologne and Jean Marais. On the other hand, *Le Capitaine Fracasse*, made by Abel Gance in 1942, proved feeble. Continental's *Premier Rendezvous*, produced by Henri Decoin and starring Danielle Darrieux, Fernand Ledoux, and the young Louis Jourdan, was a sparkling trifle.

3

4

1. *The "absolution" scene from* Les Anges du péché.

2. *Danielle Darrieux, Fernand Ledoux, and Louis Jourdan in* Premier Rendezvous.

3. *Danielle Darrieux.*

4. *The studio canteen during the production of* Le Capitaine Fracasse: *(left to right) Julien Duvivier, Assia Noris, Abel Gance, and Roland Toutain.*

5. L'Éternal Retour *with Madeleine Sologne and Jean Marais as a modern-day Tristan and Yseult.*

6. Des Jeunes Filles dan la nuit, *with Elina Labourdette and Sophie Desmarets.*

5

6

The Show Goes On

1

Parisians flocked to the theaters as well, generating tax receipts two and a half times greater than before the war, though the price of admission was now lower. The biggest attractions were well-known playwrights and actors: the melodramas of Edouard Bourdet or the comedies of Marcel Achard and particularly Sacha Guitry, whose performances ranged from magnificent to deplorable. Giraudoux staged his *Sodome et Gomorrhe*, a variation on the theme of sexual fidelity. Raimu was winning new laurels at the Comédie Française, notably in a revival of *Le Bourgeois Gentilhomme*. At the Théâtre de la Cité, Charles Dullin offered a much-admired interpretation of Harpagon, in a revival of Molière's *L'Avare*, and in 1943 he staged *Les Mouches*, an unusual play by Jean-Paul Sartre which evoked very mixed reactions. This was the age of the understudy, and behind Julien Bertheau, Jean-Louis Barrault, Madeleine Renaud, Renée Faure, and Marie Bell loomed Maria Casarès, Serge Reggiani, and Gérard Philipe. The twenty-seven-year-old Jean Vilar formed his first theatrical company, while Anouilh, Sartre (*Huis clos* appeared in 1944), and Camus with *Le Malentendu* were breathing new life into a venerated art form with productions that triumphed even over power cuts.

1. *The Café de la Régence, opposite the Comédie Française whose actors gathered there after the show. Here we see Maurice Escande and (wearing a hat) Fanny Robiane.*

2. *Charles Dullin (facing camera) at the Théâtre de la Cité for a rehearsal of* L'Avare *in May 1941.*

3. *A soup kitchen (1942) in front of the theatrical posters on the Boulevard Rochechouart.*

4. *Gérard Philipe and Dany Robin, the day of the Prix du Conservatoire award.*

5. *Gisèle Pascal applying her makeup by candlelight during a 1944 power cut.*

6. *Serge Reggiani receiving the congratulations of the cast after being awarded the Prix du Conservatoire.*

3

4

5

6

Theatrical Hits

Three plays became smash hits with both le Tout-Paris and the German *gratin*. First, in 1942, came *La Reine morte* with a cast headed by Madeleine Renaud, Julien Bertheau, Renée Faure, and Jean Yonnel. Here, Henry de Montherlant, author of *Les Jeunes Filles*, plunged into tragedy, with a plot that turned on a royal command to kill the woman for whom the King's son had defied rank in order to take as his secret wife. Then came the momentous opening, on November 26, 1943, of Paul Claudel's *Le Soulier de satin*, originally written forty years earlier but never staged. Jean-Louis Vaudoyer (Jacques Copeau's successor as director of the Comédie-Française) and Jean-Louis Barrault exerted prodigies of diplomacy to persuade the Master of Brangues that his favorite play could be successfully performed in five hours rather than ten. Reduced to a mere thirty-three changes of scene, *The Satin Slipper* unfolded with Madeleine Renaud and Jean-Louis Barrault moving between the Most Catholic King of Spain, Africa, and the New World, always to music by Arthur Honegger. In 1944, Anouilh's *Antigone* opened at the Théâtre de l'Atelier with Monelle Valentin in the title role. It demonstrated, in the manner of Sophocles, that there would always be an Antigone to rebel against the State, here personified by Creon, King of Thebes (played by Jean Davy). It was a timely thesis.

1

2

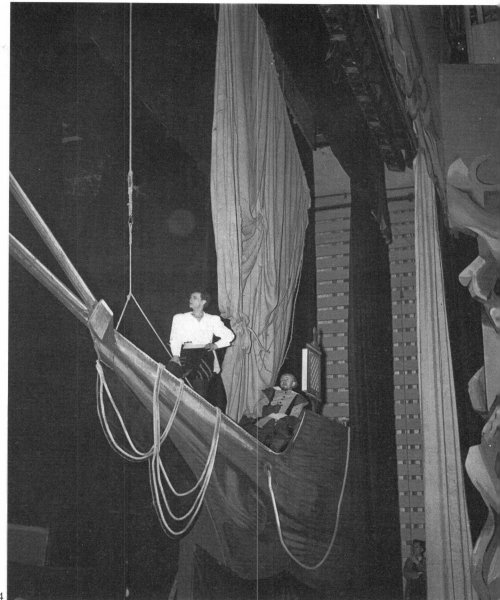

1. La Reine morte *at the Comédie-Française: (left to right)* Madeleine Renaud, Julien Bertheau, *and* Henry de Montherlant.

2. *The December 1943 (no. 12) issue of the clandestine journal* Les Lettres Françaises.

3. Le Soulier de satin, *with Madeleine Renaud in the role of Dona Musique.*

4. *Jean-Louis Barrault as Don Rodrigue in* Le Soulier de satin.

5. Antigone *at the Atelier, with Monelle Valentin and (left) M. Beauchamp.*

Literary Lights

To publish or not to publish while controled by the Occupier? That may have been the question, but there were too many who, like Jean Guéhenno, chose to lock their manuscripts in a drawer pending the return of better times. Moreover, publishing flourished, for while paper may have been scarce, copy was plentiful. Far be it from the elite intelligentsia to congregate underground. Within the magic triangle defined by the Deux Magots, the Café de Flore, and the Brasserie Lipp (still under the genial tutelage of "Papa Cazes," the best-educated illiterate on the Boulevard Saint-Germain), the comings and goings, the ideological give and take never ceased among those who would await the end of the war to settle their bloody accounts. In plate 1 Maurice Fombeure, who wanted to "protect our rights to fantasy and the autonomous act," may be recognized by his pipe and Ramon Fernandez by his spectacles. All the while, not far away, Sartre was finding inspiration in a café table for *L'Être et le Néant*. Sartre's play *Les Mouches* emerged as one of the big hits of 1943, and at the time nobody saw fit to comment on the irony of a French play performed before German officers in a theater stripped of its Jewish name: Sarah Bernhardt.

1. *The Brasserie Lipp, 1943: Cazes père and fils (both standing), Maurice Fombeure (lighting his pipe), and Ramon Fernandez (opposite).*

2. *The Brasserie Lipp.*

3. *The Café de Flore, 1943: (left to right) Yves Deniaud, Maurice Bacquet, Marianne Hardy, Raymond Bussières, Annette Poivre, and Roger Pigaut, with Jean-Paul Sartre at the next table.*

1. *The Café des Deux-Magots, 1943.*

2. *Colette at the Palais-Royal.*

3. *Paul Valéry reading his poetry at a Left Bank literary salon.*

4. *Jean Cocteau at the Palais-Royal, 1942.*

Cocteau and Colette

Colette and Cocteau dealt so little with current events that their wartime works almost seem to belong to an earlier period. Yet, the Palais-Royal, where they had their respective apartments, teemed with Germans no less than with cats. Colette published *Gigi* but also wrote for *Combat*, the Militia weekly. In fact, she dared not be overly principled, since her Jewish husband, though released after arrest, lived in constant danger, and her daughter had joined the Resistance. Cocteau also left a deliberately confused trail, reading *Renaud et Armide* to an enthralled Gerhard Heller in 1941, but later putting up a stout defense of Jean Genet when the latter fell under grave suspicion. *Les Parents terribles*, starring Jean Marais, was closed by the authorities after LVF bullies attacked the author on the Champs-Élysées. In 1944, even a revival of Racine's *Andromaque* was deemed lacking in respect owed to *le patrimoine national*. It is difficult to pass judgment on the behavior of the little world of literary Paris. Sacha Guitry, for example, claimed the Resistance mantle for having "entertained the French people in those tragic times."

3

4

Immortal Chansonniers

There were plenty of songs and of every sort. Vichy France found herself serenaded by Dassary and Maurice Chevalier in *Ça sent si bon la France*, while every night Suzy Solidor enriched her cabaret repertoire with *Lili Marlene*, the marching song of the Afrika Corps. More sensitive to present reality were the occasional songs composed for the absent prisoners of war, whom Léo Marjane remembered while humming *Je suis seul ce soir*. Romance continued to thrive, and in this domaine Charles Trenet proved peerless in songs like *Bonsoir, jolie Madame* or when posing such age-old questions as *Que reste-t-il de nos amours?* Though swing loomed large on the wartime hit parade, it had to leave room for Édith Piaf (now seated at the piano and no longer a street *môme*) and for the more serious and melancholy Trenet, as well as for the inescapable Maurice Chevalier, who after the Liberation made haste to launch into the manly, patriotic strains of *Fleur de Paris*. Did he really have to sing under the Occupation?

1

2

1. *Édith Piaf with Jean Chevrier and (right) H. Contet, who wrote the lyrics for many of her songs.*

2. *Suzy Solidor.*

3. *Maurice Chevalier.*

4. *Rehearsing a song in 1944: André Claveau at the piano with Marie-José to his right.*

5. *Singers gather opposite the Gare de Lyon at the Café de la Poste, which belonged to Eddie Barclay's father, to hear forbidden records smuggled in from Switzerland: Georges Guétary, Eddie Barclay, and (in a white hat) Suzy Solidor.*

1. *Édouard Pignon took up residence in the studio of his friend the Jewish sculptor Jacques Lipchitz, who had fled to the United States. To protect Lipchitz' works, Pignon buried them in the garden. Hostile to Collaboration, he also joined the National Committee of the Resistance.*

2. *Pablo Picasso in his studio on the Rue des Grands-Augustins.*

3. *A still life by Pignon, 1941.*

4. *In Picasso's studio, June 16, 1944, after reading the artist's little farce entitled* Le Désir attrapé par la queue.

4

Art without Joy

The graphic arts did not fare particularly well during the early 1940s. Both the Independent and the Autumn Salons continued to be held, but important new talent failed to emerge, even though "Twenty Young Painters of the French Tradition," including Jean Bazaine, Alfred Manessier, and Édouard Pignon, organized an exhibition of their work at the Galerie Braun in May 1941. While Parisians viewed the show as a reaffirmation of French taste in the face of the Nazis' preference for kitsch, like that in the "heroic" marble nudes of Arno Breker, the Germans

allowed it to open in the hope that French "decadence" would now be revealed for all to see. The works of "investment-grade" artists, such as Utrillo, Vlaminck, and van Dongen, sold well, to say nothing of Henri Matisse, whose Chinese-ink and charcoal drawings were on display at the Carré Gallery in November 1941. As for Picasso, a Spanish citizen, he lay low and minded his own business, staying close to the huge, shapeless stove purchased from a collector. The great Cubist continued to paint and draw, doing a series of line illustrations for Buffon's *Natural History*. In January 1941 he even found time to

write *Le Désir attrapé par la queue* (*Desire Caught by the Tail*), a Surrealist pastiche inspired by Alfred Jarry and Guillaume Apollinaire. When given a public reading on June 16, 1944, the little farce prompted Brassaï to immortalize the event in a group photograph (plate 4) portraying many of the "actors": Jacques Lacan, Cécile Éluard, Pierre Reverdy, Louise Leiris, Picasso, Zanie de Campan, Valentine Hugo, Simone de Beauvoir, Georges Brassaï, and (sitting or squatting) Jean-Paul Sartre, Michel Leiris, and Jean Aubier.

Musical Life Flourishes

Nor did musical performance want for audiences. Music lovers desperate for pure entertainment could find it in Henri Varna's revivals of operettas like *Les Cloches de Corneville* and *Les Mousquetaires au couvent*, while the more sophisticated went as often as possible to the ever-packed Palais Garnier, there attending performances of operas by Mozart, Richard Strauss, and even Wagner, whose *Tristan und Isolde* the French dramatic soprano Germaine Lubin sang in German. In February 1943 came the premiere of a strange, operatic *Antigone*. Staged by Jean Cocteau, it proved remarkable less for Honegger's score than for the Red-Indian-like headdresses that Cocteau had devised for the Theban warriors. It was also at the Palais Garnier that 613 singers and instrumentalists joined under the baton of Charles Münch to perform Berlioz' *Requiem*. The Jeune France group of composers, formed by Yves Baudrier, Daniel Lesur, Olivier Messiaen, and André Jolivet, collaborated on an oratorio for the feast of Saint Joan of Arc. Younger music lovers satisfied their need for live performances through membership in the Jeunesses Musicales, founded in 1942 by René Nicoly for high-school students. By 1944 the organization boasted 50,000 members in and around Paris, and 150,000 throughout France.

1. *André Jolivet.*

2. *Jacques Chaillot, one of the seven composers commissioned to write an oratorio for the feast of Saint Joan of Arc.*

3. Antigone *by Honegger and Cocteau at the Opéra, January 1943, with Hélène Bouvier and José Beckman.*

4. *Violinist Jacques Thibaud, 1942.*

5. Berlioz' Requiem *performed at the Opéra (for the first time precisely as directed by the composer) with chorus and orchestra of 613, all conducted by Charles Münch.*

6. *Germaine Lubin, much admired (by Hitler among others) for her Wagnerian performances, sang Isolde at Bayreuth in 1939.*

7. *Herbert von Karajan with Germaine Lubin, May 1941. The young conductor had come to Paris for the first time with the Berlin Opera. Sponsored by the German Institute, he would conduct a special performance of* Tristan und Isolde *on the anniversary of Wagner's birth. Singing the lead roles in the German-language production were France's Germaine Lubin and Germany's Max Lorenz.*

8. *French pianist Alfred Cortot (right) in conversation with a German singer.*

4

5

6

7

8

Lifar Leads the Dance

The Germans were great balleto-manes, usually buying a third of the seats for every performance, and they particularly admired Serge Lifar, the ballet master at the Opéra. This onetime star of Diaghilev's Ballets Russes choreographed three-quarters of the ballets performed at the Palais Garnier. Yet, he also nurtured the Russian and Spanish classics, while continuing to enrich the repertoire with his own work, such as *Les Animaux modèles*, based on La Fontaine and a score by Francis Poulenc. In plate 3 Lifar can be seen rehearsing Yvette Chauviré and in plate 4 dancing with prima ballerina Solange Schwarz in Werner Egk's *Joan de Zarissa*, a version of the Don Juan legend set in Renaissance Flanders. Meanwhile, dance lovers found plenty of promising new talent to applaud: Janine Charrat, Roland Petit, Ludmilla Tcherina, and Renée Jeanmaire. Whatever its deficiencies, the period did not lack grace.

1. *Desty and his "speaking chorus."*

2. *Dancers Janine Charrat and Roland Petit posing for Christian Bérard.*

3. *In the foyer of the Paris Opéra, Serge Lifar corrects an attitude struck by Yvette Chauviré.*

4. *Serge Lifar and Solange Schwarz in* Joan de Zarissa.

5. *Set for* Les Animaux modèles *danced to music by Francis Poulenc, August 1942.*

6. *Serge Lifar and the Opéra corps de ballet.*

3

4

5

6

1

2   3

Radio Waves

Radio-Paris and Radiodiffusion Nationale (which maintained four studios in the capital) competed for the Parisian audience, offering variety shows, serials (many of them based on the detective stories of Georges Siménon), advice on everyday problems (with André Claveau making a fool of himself in *Cette Heure est à vous*, a program aimed at women), and sports. In the afternoon the two stations featured musical or cultural programs, like Schaeffer's experimental broadcasts or literary ones on the order of Max de Rieux's series called "Their Debuts," in which Madeleine Renaud, Sacha Guitry, Noël Roquevert, Jean Desailly, and many others helped launch onto the airwaves the first efforts by a writer or a performer. France had been experimenting with television as early as 1933, but the war halted all such activity, until the Germans resumed transmissions for the benefit of their hospitalized wounded and allowed a few favored Parisians to watch as well. During the Occupation the star newscaster was Howard Vernon, a Swiss with perfect bilingual command of both German and French.

4

1. *The first wartime telecast in France.*

2. *Radiodiffusion Nationale's "Their Debuts" broadcast from Sacha Guitry's house: (left to right) François Périer, Geneviève de Serreville, and Sacha Guitry.*

3. *Madeleine Renaud and Jean Desailly reading Alfred de Musset's* Il ne faut jurer de rien *from Radiodiffusion Nationale's Paris studio, November 1943.*

4. *At home with Sacha Guitry, surrounded by Noël Roquevert, Geneviève de Serreville, and François Périer.*

5. *In Radiodiffusion Nationale's experimental studio, an engineer shows an apprentice how to position the cutting head on a recording device, while Pierre Schaeffer looks on, May 1943.*

5

1

2

3

4

5

6

Haute Couture for Wartime

As early as October 1940, the winter haute couture collections began to worry the authorities. Not only were German officers buying costly ensembles for their wives, thereby questioning the taste of Berlin, but, moreover, the fashion industry pretended that it was saving the honor of Paris and its style from the slings and arrows of outrageous fortune. This seemed a bit presumptuous, and so it was decided that models, or designs, should be limited to seventy-five per collection. In addition, it was urged that forms not be made too full. And couturiers did indeed adjust to circumstances, recommending, for instance, that only the hostess wear a long dress, while her guests appear in well-made but short creations. They also remembered that the well-dressed lady might have to travel by velo and thus offered her an imaginative line of sportswear. Since the winter would be harsh, they counseled long sleeves and linings. Meanwhile, designers could—thank God!—make up for all the austerity by lavishing their attention on hats. Exploding with charm, fantasy, and amplitude, all crafted with every possible or imaginable material and tilted jauntily forward, wartime Parisian millinery defied the fanatics of textile economy.

1. *A Jacques Fath ensemble,* La Femme Chic, *January 1943.*

2. *A design by Germaine Leconte, September 1942.*

3. *A dress from Germaine Leconte, with a hat by Rose Valois,* La Femme Chic, *May 1942.*

4. *Germaine Leconte, February 1942.*

5. *An ensemble from Nina Ricci, worn by the model Gabrielle in January 1943.*

6. *An ensemble from Nina Ricci, worn by Roberte in October 1942.*

7. *The models' dressing room.*

8. *Fashions from Jean Patou, 1941.*

9. *La mode "vélo" in 1940.*

10. *Designs by Schiaparelli, 1943.*

7

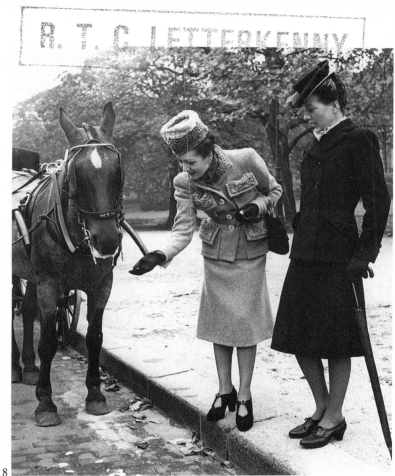

8

9

10

131

French Prisoners Disappear

The Battle of France ended so messily that the conqueror succeeded in taking a good many prisoners. Then, contrary to all the rules of war, the Germans continued to "take prisoners" even after the armistice had been signed at Rethondes. For the Reich, prisoners constituted invaluable political hostages, and some 1.5 million of them wound up in Oflags (for officers) and Stalags. In Paris, meanwhile, mothers, wives, girl friends, and kin gathered outside the Pensions Ministry in the Rue de Bellechasse to inquire after their vanished loved ones. The first lists of wounded and captured appeared in July, after which a National Information Center was set up, with a filing system installed in one of the reading rooms of the Archives Nationales. Those who slipped through the net made their way home by special train, in civilian clothes or with a white armband, all bearing a stamped official certificate of discharge. These lucky veterans could not yet know that they had escaped five years of captivity.

1. *A file room at the National Information Center in the Archives Nationales.*

2. *Outside the Pensions Ministry in the Rue de Bellechasse, a crowd waits in July 1940 for lists of the missing, the wounded, the dead, and those held prisoner in Germany.*

3. *In July 1940 a civilian information center was established in the Chamber of Deputies.*

4. *Demobilized soldiers outside the Gare du Nord.*

5. *Demobilized soldiers arriving at the Gare d'Austerlitz.*

6. *Distribution of the first official lists of the missing and the imprisoned, July 25, 1940.*

4

5

6

Refugees Return

The Occupier quickly tired of the hue and cry over the chaos stemming from the invasion, and after a few weeks decided to assist the hordes of Exodus refugees to return home. Simultaneously, they also used the occasion to fuel the propaganda machine, pasting their infamous poster on every wall: "Abandoned populations...trust the German soldier." The first to return, with their wheelbarrows and baby carriages, were those who had not been able to get very far. Then, as a matter of urgent priority, came the convoys of trucks bearing police, railroad men, and postal workers. On July 7 an official report held that Paris could count a population of 1,051,306, which still left the capital pretty well deserted from the Place de la Concorde to the Porte Maillot. By October 22 the number had risen to 1,910,000, and it was estimated that in the single week of August 4–11, 350,000 Parisians re-entered their city by train. If the municipality's figures can be believed, the population on January 1, 1942, had regained the prewar total of 2,778,533 souls, a level that soon subsided as the city lost some half-million people, including Jews rounded up and those conscripted for labor in Germany. Others left in search of friendlier climes, and perhaps they were right.

1. *Belgian refugees awaiting repatriation outside the Gare du Nord, July 1940.*

2, 4, 5, 6, 7. *Refugees struggling back from the Exodus.*

3. *Torn German poster, July 1940.*

2

3

4

5

6

7

1

A Superficial Continuity

Scarcely had the advance units of the Wehrmacht passed through Paris than cabarets, nightclubs, and music halls reopened, with movie and legitimate theaters following suit in mid-July. *L'Oeuvre* had already recommenced publishing on July 11. The authorities—French as well as German—strove to restore the capital to its outward appearance before the war. Even the sandbags were removed so that the great door of Notre-Dame could once again be admired. The Bourse renewed trading on October 14, 1940, an event hailed as a symbol of the turn to normalcy, though activity was limited to French government bonds, and margin trades could no longer be negotiated. But such was the disarray in French commerce during the fall of 1940 that department stores and other businesses reduced their staffs. To keep them busy, the unemployed were set to work repaving streets.

1. *The Paris Bourse. In the foreground, the* corbeil *or "basket" where brokers trade only for cash; in the background, a group of specialists keeping track of the trades.*

2

2. *Inspection at the entrance to the Bourse, April 26, 1941.*

3. *Notice to owners of safe-deposit boxes, which could be opened only in the presence of the Occupier.*

4. *June 28, 1940.*

5. *The great door of Notre-Dame being cleared of sandbagging.*

3

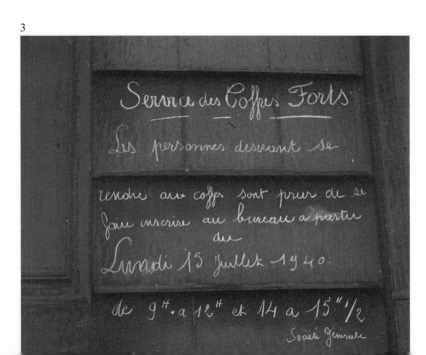

4

5

A Fight for Food

Needless to say, Parisians under the Occupation spent much of their energy just finding fuel for the stove and food for the pot. Military constraints and the tight blockade imposed by the Royal Navy, which cut off trade between France and her overseas empire, produced shortages that the Occupier's levies could only make worse. While the authorities, for political reasons, needed to save Parisians from actual malnutrition, the capital nonetheless remained uncomfortably dependent on its hinterland. In 1938 Parisians had consumed 66,000 tons of meat, while their total allotment for 1942 was 26,000 tons, for 1943 only 23,000 tons, and for 1944 less than 20,000 tons. Beef continued to trickle in somehow or another, but supplies of veal, and even more particularly pork, dried up, from 118,000 hogs shipped to the slaughterhouses in 1938 to just 6,840 in 1944. Vegetables too were in short supply, and the 129,000 tons handled at Les Halles in 1938 dwindled to 80,500 in 1942, 60,000 in 1943, and 40,000 in 1944. The much-sought-after turnip sold at a premium on the black market, prompting the Prefect of the Seine to prohibit the shipping of rutabagas—those yellow root vegetables that came to symbolize the empty stomach of the Occupation years—from his jurisdiction.

1, 2. *Parisians lugging sacks of potatoes on the Métro.*

3, 4. *The markets of Les Halles.*

5. *Cattle at the Porte d'Orléans being herded to the slaughterhouse.*

6. *Returning from market.*

l'Humanité

Fondateur : JEAN-JAURÈS
Rédacteur en chef : VAILLANT-
(1926-1937) COUTURIER

ORGANE CENTRAL DU PARTI COMMUNISTE FRANÇAIS (S.F.I.C.) N° 163 - 22 MAI 1942.

Laval-la-famine diminue la ration de pain.

Le "ganleiter" Laval imposé par Hitler et nommé par Pétain, veut que notre blé soit livré aux boches en plus grandes quantités. Pour cela, il réduit notre ration de pain, si cruellement insuffisante, mais ce bandit n'ose pas dire ce qu'il nous prépare. Cependant, il ressort des déclarations officielles volontairement embrouillées, qu'à partir du 1er Juin, la ration des adultes sera réduite de 25 grs par jour et la ration des tout petits enfants, celle des vieux, des adolescents, des travailleurs et des cultivateurs sera réduite de 40 grs par jour. Que la journée des Mères, le 31 Mai, veille de l'entrée en vigueur de ces décrets de famine, soit le point de départ d'une vigoureuse campagne de manifestations populaires contre les affameurs. Mères de famille, prenez la tête du combat contre Laval-la-Famine.

Manifestez, exigez du pain, du pain, du pain! Pas de blé pour les boches! Du pain pour les Français!

La main tendue aux catholiques

Bien avant la guerre, alors que l'hitlérisme menaçait notre pays, le Parti Communiste Français, par la voix de Maurice THOREZ, s'adressa directement aux catholiques, et leur tendit une main fraternelle en vue d'unir tous les hommes de bonne volonté contre l'ennemi commun. Le Parti Communiste fut combattu par les uns, raillé par les autres pour avoir osé poser publiquement le problème de l'alliance indispensable entre croyants et athées, mais il ne se laissa rebuter par rien dans son œuvre d'union du peuple français contre le fascisme barbare, et les évènements d'aujourd'hui montrent combien il avait raison. Dans leur immense masse, les catholiques sont patriotes et ils ne s'inclinent pas devant les oppresseurs de notre pays, dont la victoire passagère ne fut possible que grâce à la complicité de la 5ème colonne hitlérienne en France.

2

Qui fait le Marché noir ?

Le marché noir ne peut se faire qu'avec le concours d[es] Allemands dont les camions peuvent, seuls, circuler sa[ns] contrôle. Il faut donc chercher les trafiquants du marché no[ir] parmi les collaborateurs et amis des boches.

Voici les noms de quelques trafiquants haut placés qui s'e[n]richissent de la misère du peuple, de l'asservissement de [la] France et donnent tout son sens à la fameuse « Révolution N[a]tionale » dont la devise pourrait être : VOL, TRAHISON[,] ESCLAVAGE.

3

Rationing and Famine

Shortages meant rationing, and the first cards appeared on September 23, 1940. A month later a classification system went into effect. Strictly enforced, it took account of age and supposed nutritional needs: E for children less than three years old; JI, children 3–6; J2, children 6–13; J3 (a much-debated category), adolescents 13–21; A, adults 25–70; V, the elderly over 70. There were also sub-classifications, such as T for adult workers, T1 and T2 for manual laborers; FE for pregnant women; FA for women breast-feeding babies. Issued in the bearer's name, the ration cards, with their sheets of varicolored coupons identified by letters and numbers, came under the control of the "nutrition service," a bureaucracy of 9,000 employees. It urged citizens to read their newspapers for notification of the day on which a particular commodity would be distributed. On the designated day people took their places in queues, those homes away from home so closely associated with the wartime era of hardship and humiliation. Since the Occupier distrusted crowds, the queue could not be formed more than half an hour before the opening of the store, where another tyrant, feared and envied, reigned supreme—the butcher or the dairyman. The underground press railed against the gray-green-clad Krauts and their accomplice, the famine-monger Laval.

1. *The underground l'Humanité for May 22, 1942, exhorting Parisians to demonstrate against new starvation cuts planned for the bread ration, all the while that French wheat was being shipped to Germany.*

2. *Leaflet attacking the black market and the involvement of Germans and Collaborationists in it. "We know," it concludes, "what the famous 'National Revolution' stands for. It stands for THEFT, TREASON, AND SLAVERY."*

3. *Les Halles on "butter day."*

4. *Queue outside a bakery, 1943.*

5. *Queuing to buy vegetables.*

6. *Food shop window, 1944.*

Days Without

To make shortages look more equitable, restaurants were required to observe a "day without" three times a week—that is, without meat or even without liquor. The great temples of gluttony, of course, could scarcely have been expected to bother about such tedious measures, and they always managed to serve one's favorite champagne or real coffee. At the corner bistro, however, one had to be content with "national coffee," a brew totally innocent of the bean, to which many customers preferred a cup of *viandox* or beef broth. The "parallel market," a kind of small-scale black market, thrived on desperation and a growing sense of unfairness. Needless to say, the prices there rose above official ceilings, and barter came into frequent practice. The authorities struggled in vain to exercise some degree of control, by requiring, for example, that worn-out possessions, such as light bulbs, be exchanged for new ones. An order of January 23, 1941, made it unlawful to "discard, burn, or destroy, except for reasons of public health, metal scrap, old paper, feathers, rubber, bones, hides, or hair." Another decree, issued on March 27, improved on the earlier one by prescribing methods for salvaging "horns, hooves, and horseshoes." Life became an unequal race between the rich—old and new—who could buy pretty much whatever they liked, and the ordinary ruck of humanity who tried to survive by the grace of system D.

142

1. *Restrictions—a no-liquor day.*

2. *A restaurant employee in search of fish, 1943.*

3. *French fries on sale at Les Halles.*

4. *Chalkboard in a food shop, announcing what could be provided against ration coupons.*

5, 6. *Petty merchants at Les Halles.*

1. *Making vitamin-enriched candies.*

2. *A butcher at Les Halles distributing hot soup to the hungry, February 1941.*

3. *Raimu and Maupi passing out cookies at Les Halles, April 1944.*

4. *1941: Artists could dine every night at Pomme on the Rue Tholozé in Montmartre. Here, the Spanish painter Craixam sits with his back to the camera, flanked by the art dealer Coste on his left and Gen Paul on his right.*

5. *At the Secours National, soup for young mothers, 1942.*

6. *Nursery-school children being served soup for lunch.*

5

Soup Kitchens

To satisfy the most elementary needs, palliatives had to be found. They came from quickly mobilized civic services and certain private foundations—the Secours Nationale, for instance—heavily subsidized by public funds. Not only did communal soup kitchens continue; there would also be, beginning in December 1942, the "rescos," restaurants where families with incomes of less than 3,000 francs a year could buy meals at very low prices. The rescos might serve as many as 50,000 meals a day. The government demonstrated its professed esteem for mothers by organizing special "mothers' snacks," at the same time that their children received vitamin-enriched cookies and candies. In 1944, Raimu himself took part in the distribution of these dietary supplements, thought, incorrectly, to be rich in calcium as well.

6

1

2

Le Dernier Métro

The TCRP (Transports en Commun de la Région Parisienne, or Paris Regional Public Transportation) was hard put to move Parisians about. At rush hours one needed the skills of a gymnast to clamber aboard a gas-powered bus swollen like a gigantic balloon. Better to take one's chances on the Métro, the capital's underground lung, which moved more than a billion passengers a year, selling an average of 2.5 million tickets a day in February 1941 and 3.5 million by November 1942. However, it could scarcely have been fun to shove one's way into or elbow free of always-packed cars, while the Wehrmacht rode free in first class. No matter—the Métro's stations and corridors were convivial places.

3

1. *The Métro station at Les Halles, 1944.*

2. *The Métro station at the Rue de Vaugirard, 1941.*

3. *German servicewomen on the Place de l'Opéra.*

4. *Actors taking the last Métro after the show. Here, Fernand Ledoux and—could it be Simone Signoret?*

Out of Circulation

The first product to be rationed was petrol, the strategic arm par excellence of that machine-driven war. Parisians soon found themselves reduced to a very short supply: 2 percent of prewar consumption. The traffic police received new gloves, which remained pristine white since there were no automobiles to control. Only 4,500 driving licenses had been issued, compared to 350,000 parking spaces. Moreover, French cars were reserved to the government, certain professions (doctors especially), and those in good standing with the Occupier. Early in the Occupation, all manner of makeshift vehicles appeared, but the bicycle soon became the conveyance of choice. The sounds of Paris were no longer the same.

1

2

1. *Parking in the Faubourg Saint-Honoré; at the left, a car equipped with a natural-gas tank.*

2. *A 402 equipped with a gas generator.*

3. *Petrol pumps.*

148

3

The Trains Get Through

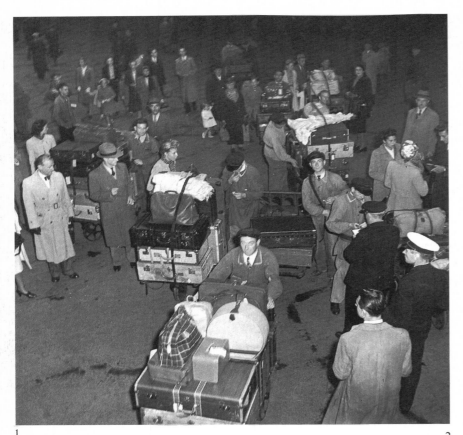

With automobile travel sharply curtailed, Parisians needing to travel any great distance had to depend on the railways, which also carried 80 percent of the freight destined for the capital. The stations were crowded, especially on Sunday, but once passengers had checked their bicycles through, they could fall to dreaming about all the provisions they could bring back from the country, prizes that made tolerable the journey in crowded, notoriously uncomfortable trains. Returning home usually involved inspections and searches, with baggage opened to check for underground newspapers and leaflets, even though the contents might be more down-to-earth things. Those fortunate enough not to come back empty-handed, and also not to have trouble at the check point, would scarcely have dared to entrust their precious cargo to a porter.

1. *Porters servicing passengers just arrived by train.*

2. *At the Gare de l'Est in 1940, handcarts replaced cabs for transporting baggage.*

3. *Bicycles and baggage at the Gare Saint-Lazare in July 1940.*

4. *A Youth Workshop.*

5. *Variety artists opening a student canteen, September 1941: (left to right) Johnny Hess, Lys Gauty, Élyane Célis, Charpini.*

6. *A Youth Workshop being opened on the Rue Clavel, May 1941.*

4

5

6

La Jeunesse du Maréchal

Vichy evinced great solicitude towards the young, whom it regarded as sufficiently malleable to become a force capable of bringing about the National Revolution. Youth loomed large in public debate, and in August 1941 this segment of the population received a good slice of the National Lottery. The most urgent problem was the high level of unemployment among adolescents—about 400,000 in November 1940 but only 40,000 two years later. To help the jobless young, some sixty *Centres d'Accueil*, or Reception Centers, which also functioned as trade schools, opened in Paris. Although the Occupation authorities approved of this development, they nonetheless issued an order on August 29, 1940, prohibiting mass-membership youth organizations in the Occupied Zone, where the potential for generating nationalist sentiments seemed too great. Neither Boy Scouts nor *Chantiers de Jeunesse* (Youth Workshops) would be allowed. The Germans made an exception only for *La Jeunesse du Maréchal*, a small Pétainist group over which they could exert indirect control, and for the "national teams" organized to render narrowly defined social service, which would indeed be needed in the aftermath of air raids.

1

2

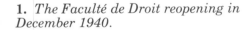

3

The military debacle of 1940 disrupted the examination timetable, so that the candidates for university entrance (seen leaving the Lycée Saint-Louis in plate 2) sat for their first papers at the end of July. Oral examinations had been omitted, and the results of the written tests would not be published until September. Thereafter, school life resumed its habitual round, though the National Ministry of Education distributed new instructions consistent with the ideology of the National Revolution. Also, principals solemnly read aloud "messages" from Marshal Pétain to high-school students, who were fewer than before the war (25,000 against 35,000). And like other Parisians, they had to contend with cold and hunger. Hardly reopened, classes closed again on November 11, 1940, when hundreds of lycée and college students demonstrated along the Champs-Élysées. The Faculté de Droit, or Law School, did not reopen until December 20. At the venerable Sorbonne something new had been added: two chairs for the scientific (*sic*) study of Judaism.

1. *The Faculté de Droit reopening in December 1940.*

2. *The Boulevard Saint-Michel after the college entrance examinations.*

3. *Marshal Pétain's "message" being read to students at a Paris lycée.*

4. *The Deligny swimming pool in 1944.*

152

4

153

Amor Vincit Omnia

The war, the prisoners, and the STO, or forced labor, all worked against matrimony, and the number of marriages celebrated in Paris declined from more than 29,000 in 1939 to fewer than 15,000 in 1943. Legal marriages between Germans and Frenchwomen—or yet between Frenchmen and German service-women, the so-called "gray mice"—occurred so rarely as to be almost countable on the fingers of two hands. There were 104 mixed marriages in 1939, 25 in 1941, 12 in 1943, and 9 in 1944. The bride and groom seen in plate 1, arriving at the Madeleine Church, both hailed from across the Rhine. By contrast, French weddings, apart from the inescapable white for the bride, became shabbier and shabbier. The soprano Géori Boué, who had just made her debut at the Opéra, and Roger Bourdin, fresh from a triumphant concert at the Salle Favart, could manage a formal wedding even in May 1944. Ordinary people, however, had to make do with the least of means.

1. *A German wedding at the Madeleine Church.*

2. *The wedding of Géori Boué and Roger Bourdin in May 1944, with Gaby Morlay in attendance.*

3

Worship God, Not Heroes

In the troubled years of the Occupation, Church Holy Days were celebrated with more than customary fervor. Sometimes, however, the war made it necessary to alter the timetable, as for the Christmas Midnight Mass, which, owing to curfew, was celebrated around 5 PM at Saint-Sulpice as well as at all other churches in the capital. What the Wehrmacht and Vichy alike would not tolerate was any observance of July 14, Bastille Day, or November 11, Armistice Day marking the end of World War I and the Allied victory over Imperial Germany. Given this prohibition, certain Parisiennes took pride, at the appropriate moments, in wearing ensembles composed of red, white, and blue. On the other hand, one could, on the proper Feast Day, parade unmolested before the statue of Joan of Arc at the Place des Pyramides. Between the two World Wars this Saint had been more or less co-opted by the extreme right, after which Vichy made her a kind of patroness of the nation, a model for all to follow. Moreover, it had been the English, not the Germans, whom the Maid of Orléans fought— no small virtue in the eyes of the Occupier.

4

3. *In 1940, Christmas Mass at Saint-Sulpice, celebrated at 5 in the afternoon because of curfew.*

4. *Schoolchildren returning to Paris in August 1940 pay their respects at the Tomb of the Unknown Soldier.*

Sporting Life

When the racetracks reopened, Parisians thronged to the Sunday pari-mutuel in the hope of sweetening their monthly pay check. Betting in 1943 was five times higher than in 1938. With the coming of good weather, Parisians could also make Sunday bicycle trips to the Bois de Boulogne. Those with presentable figures packed the Deligny pool and the artificial beach near the Pont d'Iéna on the site of the 1937 World's Fair. Although reserving certain open spaces for military training, the Occupier permitted a normal level of traditional sports, and soccer, cycling, and swimming remained as popular as ever. There appeared an unusual variety of umpire—a huge photograph of Philippe Pétain, to which competitors at the Parc des Princes swore an oath of fealty in June 1941.

1. *Sunday in the Bois.*

2. *Athletes swearing an oath before the portrait of Marshal Pétain at the Parc des Princes.*

3. *Open-air picture gallery in Montparnasse.*

4. *On the Champs-Élysées.*

5. *Betting at the racetrack.*

6. *Philatelists' market in the Champs-Élysées gardens.*

5

6

Foraging for Coal

Alump of coal—this became the most treasured of all commodities during the Occupation. It lay utterly beyond the reach of individuals, since coal constituted one of the sinews of war. For this very reason, the Militärfehlshaber in Brussels took control of the mines in northeastern France, which had traditionally supplied Paris, and allowed only a trickle of coal to reach the rest of the country. The capital saw not a kilo during the big chill of 1940–41, except by way of the black market, and between 1941 and 1944 Paris received only two allocations, each consisting of three tons per family. To obtain more of the precious fuel, one had to tramp over dumps and gather bits by hand. As for wood, there was no allotment whatever, other than to bakers, who claimed all of it. Sawdust stoves, despite their cumbersomeness, found a certain favor. The more imaginative among the cold-natured tried to develop a portable stove buring papier-mâché, but richly ingenious as this technology may have been, it delivered rather poor rewards.

1

2

1. *Desperate people gathering fuel at Argenteuil, September 1940.*

2. *Ashcans sometimes yielded a bit of coke.*

Cruel Winters

During the Occupation, Parisians had the worst possible luck with the weather. Virtually all the winters proved harsh, bringing exceptionally low temperatures, and that of 1940–41 broke every record with its seventy days below freezing (twenty more than normal), regularly dropping to 7°F, not counting the wind-chill factor. In January 1942 skiers took to the slopes of Montmartre, and while the cold abated somewhat in 1942–43, it returned with a vengeance in 1943–44, again trying both body and spirit, through long, weary months when it seemed that the war would never end. As a matter of habit, one kept to the least frigid, most insulated room available, and in poorer quarters neighbors took turns gathering round in one another's apartments in order to get the most from their lukewarm stoves.

3

4

3. *The Occupation was accompanied by the harshest of winters.*

4. *Lycée Rollin students on their way to collect clothing.*

Blackouts

Until 1943 Paris could count, more or less, on its regular supply of electricity. (In 1938 the capital had burned 476 kilowatts, as compared to 1943, when it consumed 442 million.) To supplement the yield of the seven coal-fired generators, the authorities tapped the hydroelectric power generated in the Massif Central. And it was the unusually low water level behind the dams that caused a total outage on the night of January 23–24, 1942. After that, strict economy reigned, which, because of the blackout, allowed little or no street lighting, a situation guaranteed nightly by meddlesome civil-defense wardens. It shut down certain Métro stations and forced all commercial theaters to close one extra day per week. Even this did not suffice, and by 1944 the power cuts had become longer and longer. In February no electricity flowed between 9 and 11 AM or between 2 and 5 PM, and in July domestic buildings received no juice at all during daytime hours, except for thirty minutes around noon. With power unavailable for driers, coiffeurs had to let their clients' hair dry outdoors. From then on, candles figured large in every prudent Parisian's bag of survival tricks.

1

1. *Getting one's hair set in the sun, 1944.*

2. *A votive candle used for lighting, 1944.*

3. *At the Daunou Theater, Gisèle Pascal and Jean Paqui perform by candlelight.*

4, 5. *Making a phone call and serving a glass of champagne by candlelight during a power cut.*

2

3

4

5

Taking Shelter

When the sirens began to wail, Parisians had about fifteen minutes in which to take shelter. The protection offered by cellars may have been more imaginary than real, in the event a bomb exploded nearby. Still, people went there rather than leave their homes. Some hospitals finally set up public wards underground. The authorities recommended that Parisians repair to approved shelters, where teachers were required to lead their classes if an alert came during the day. At night the shelters had their "regulars" who virtually claimed title to certain spaces. Stimulated by fear of a direct hit from an incendiary bomb, they all cohabited in a strange kind of conviviality. The deepest of the Métro stations served as shelters, which, being considered very safe, became makeshift dormitories.

1. *A plane flying over the flower market in 1944.*

2, 3. *Civil-defense posters identifying shelters and giving instructions on how to dig out in the event of a direct hit.*

4. *The Lamarck Métro station during an alert.*

4

The New "Relief" Plan

The German war machine had an insatiable appetite for foreign workers. Initially, Berlin tried to satisfy its needs by soliciting "volunteer workers," and many responded, especially the unemployed attracted by the ubiquitous posters promising good pay. But of the 200,000 or less who departed France for work in Germany, only 70,000 remained east of the Rhine by June 1942, when Hitlerian Germany began forcing the conquered—indeed vassalized—countries to pay tribute in the form of hard labor. Gauleiter Fritz Sauckel, who took charge of organizing this human export, soon came to be known as "the slave-trader of Europe." To fill his quota, he drew heavily on the skilled workers of France. Simultaneously, Laval dreamt up a "Relief" program whereby for every three jobs in which Frenchmen "relieved" Germans for duty at the Russian front, one French prisoner of war would be "relieved," or released, from his stalag.

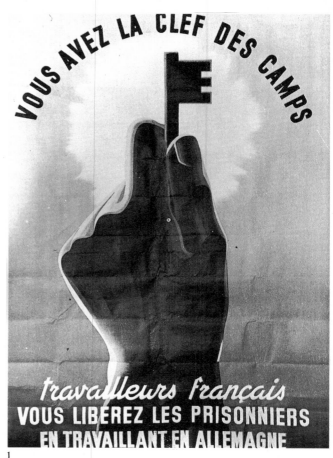

1

2

ILS DONNENT LEUR SANG

DONNEZ VOTRE TRAVAIL
pour sauver l'Europe du Bolchevisme

Slaves to Hitler

Following the almost total failure of Laval's "Relief" program of recruiting French "volunteers" to "relieve" German industrial labor, Vichy on September 4, 1942, promulgated the "law for the utilization and deployment of manual labor." This led to the mobilization of February 16, 1943, which made three classes of men—from every profession—born between January 1, 1920, and December 31, 1922, subject to duty. Thus came into being the labor draft known as the STO, or Service du Travail Obligatoire. The Parisian press, acting on orders, hastened to pretend, by means of carefully selected photos, that the departures for Germany were taking place in a spirit of joy and good humor. Nothing could have been further from the truth. The Resistance quickly acted to staunch the human hemorrhage instigated for the sake of the Reich's grand strategy. "Sabotage the conscription of slaves to Hitler," read the headline in the March 1, 1943, issue of *Libération*. Slightly more than 650,000 Frenchmen ended up in Germany, but by the autumn of 1943 there were fewer departures than defections, which in turn swelled the ranks of the Resistance, even if going underground in the capital became increasingly difficult as the months went by.

1. *Propaganda poster exhorting Frenchmen to work in Germany for the sake of "relieving" prisoners of war from Hitler's stalags.*

2. *Frenchwomen registering for work in Germany.*

3. *A propaganda poster: "They give their blood; give your labor, in order to save Europe from Bolshevism."*

4. L'Humanité, *the Communist Party's underground newspaper, for October 2, 1942, protesting the draft of French workers for labor in Germany.*

PANTAGRUEL

FEUILLE D'INFORMATIONS

«...Jamais ne se tourmentait, jamais ne se scandalisait. Ainsi eût-il été fortissu du deifique manoir de raison, si autrement se fût contristé ou altéré. Car tous les biens que le ciel couvre et que la terre contient en toutes ses dimensions ne sont dignes d'émouvoir nos affections et troubler nos sens et esprits...»

ainsi parlait PANTAGRUEL.

No 1   Oct 1940

PANTAGRUEL est une feuille d'informations et non de lutte saine contre l'Autorité occupante. Son but est la diffusion des nouvelles venues d'Angleterre par radio, dont trop de gens sont privés, et en souffrent.

Mais il est tout de même nécessaire d'indiquer clairement l'esprit qui l'anime. C'est l'espoir ardent que la victoire de l'Angleterre sauvera la France de la perte de plusieurs de ses provinces, ses colonies, de l'esclavage économique, et de l'inflation forcée.

L'Angleterre, ne l'oublions pas, a déclaré que ses buts de guerre comprenaient le rétablissement de l'intégrité territoriale de la France. C'est pourquoi nous souhaitons sa victoire et non l'anéantissement du peuple allemand dont personne ne méconnait le génie.

Nous nous efforcerons donc d'éviter toutes critiques haineuses ou acerbes contre les Allemands, par souci de cette objectivité, cette sérénité de jugement que Rabelais recommande dans les quelques lignes qui nous servent d'exergue, et aussi, pourquoi ne pas le reconnaître loyalement parce que l'attitude de nos ennemis est correcte, souvent même courtoise.

Mais, Français, comprenez bien ceci.

L'Allemand qui vous parle si cordialement éprouve peut-être une certaine sympathie pour la France, c'est le cas de bon nombre d'entre eux. Mais n'oubliez pas que la théorie du *Deutschland über alles* veut que tout soit écrasé, s'il le faut, pour la grandeur de l'Allemagne. Il approuvera sans réserve les conditions de paix draconiennes qui nous seront imposées.

L'Allemagne exige déjà de nous 400 millions par jour de frais d'occupation, soit sept fois plus que nous lui avions demandé en 1918!!! Ceci nous indique l'échelle de ses prétentions?

L'Alsace-Lorraine est un des joyaux de la France. L'Alsacien et le Lorrain sont de culture et de sentiments Français, bien que leur tempérament et leur sensibilité témoignent d'une transition entre les deux pays. Mais

The Busy Underground Press

The Resistance used every possible means to combat, among other things, the Occupier's propaganda, the Collaborationist press, and the Vichy government. In this political battle, Resisters found their principal weapons in leaflets, underground newspapers, and "shadow" publishing. In Paris leaflets were distributed in the thousands, particularly by the Communists, while France as a whole could count 1,024 clandestine publications, for the most part haphazardly issued newspapers of two or four pages. Some of them did not survive long, like *Pantagruel*, a hand-

some production whose first number appeared in October 1940. It was the work of Raymond Deiss, a well-known music publisher, who was arrested a year later and guillotined on August 24, 1943. The Resistance even had its own underground book-publishing house, aptly named Les Éditions de Minuit and run by novelist Pierre de Lescure and his friend, the engraver Jean Bruller-Vercors. The latter also wrote the first of the firm's twenty-five slim publications, *Le Silence de la mer*, which appeared in February 1942.

The Writers' Resistance

Some writers, but not the majority, joined the Resistance, after their fashion. The poet and essayist Jean Cassou put together the Musée de l'Homme group as early as 1940, before he became, following the Allied landings, Commissioner of the Republic at Toulouse. Jean Paulhan, a prewar one-man band at the Nouvelle Revue Française, was everywhere, but most particularly on the board of *Lettres Françaises*, the first number of which appeared on September 20, 1942, the anniversary of the French victory over the Prussians in 1792. Joining him on that board were the novelist Jean Blanzat and the poet Louis Aragon. Paul

Éluard made a selection of twenty-two poems from writers such as Aragon, Éluard, Guillevic, Ponge, Seghers, Tardieu, Vercors, and Desnos and published them on July 14, 1943, under the title *L'Honneur des poètes*. Desnos, after his arrest in February 1944, died of typhus in a death camp. Behind the pseudonym Forez hid François Mauriac, all the while that he wrote *Le Cahier noir*, a lucid meditation on those grim and pitiless times. Albert Camus, a much younger writer whose *L'Étranger* and *Le Mythe de Sysyphe* appeared in 1942, joined the Resistance in the fall of 1943 and became an editorial writer for *Combat*. Here, he declared, "we learn the real value of words."

5

6

7

8

1. *Jean Cassou, curator at the Musée National d'Art Moderne.*

2. *Albert Camus.*

3. *François Mauriac.*

4. *Louis Aragon.*

5. *Paul Éluard at home in the Rue Marx-Domoy, la Chapelle quarter.*

6. *Memorial plaque, 19 Rue Mazarine.*

7. *Robert Desnos in 1943, a few days before the Gestapo arrested him.*

8. *Jean Paulhan (left) and Jean Blanzat.*

1

2

3

4

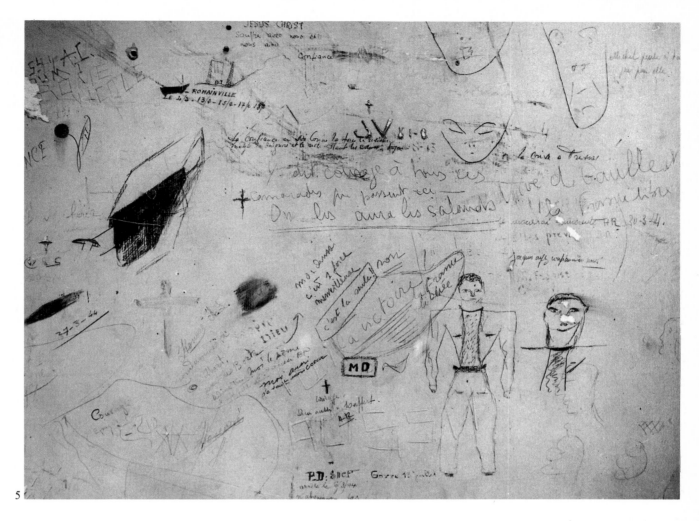

5

The Gestapo's Bathtub

The oppressors, French no less than German, strove to characterize the Resistance as a gang of "terrorists" in the pay of foreign powers. Denouncing them, the argument went, could be seen as a civic duty, the performance of which would be rewarded with cash. Resistance members "fell" as a result of imprudence or bad luck, but just as often from betrayal by an informant. And once arrested they were usually handed over to the public executioner. Paris abounded in torture chambers, with that of the Gestapo itself located on the Avenue Foch, no less. Meanwhile, in the same posh quarter, the Belgian Masuy, alias Delfanne, boasted of the "bathtub torture" he had developed and put into effect on the Avenue Henri-Martin. Here, the naked victim would be submerged in a tub filled with ice water until suffocated. The French Gestapo could easily hold its own in this deadly league. An ex-convict and his partner, the former police inspector Bonny, managed the "Rue Laur-iston Gestapo," while Berger and his henchmen carried out violent interrogations at the "Rue de la Pompe Gestapo." Often sadistic perverts, these French interrogators used physical cruelty not merely to obtain information but also to break their victim. The walls of the torture chambers bore mute witness to the unspeakable sufferings endured there.

1. *Poster offering an official million-franc reward for information leading to the arrest of saboteurs.*

2. *Handprints of torture victims on the asbestos-lined wall of a cellar in the Boulevard Victor.*

3. *Photographed the day following the Liberation, the "bathtub" at the former Ministry of the Interior on the Rue des Saussaies, which the Gestapo had requisitioned in 1940.*

4. *A Gestapo cell.*

5. *Graffiti on the wall of a Gestapo cell.*

171

1

2

3

Youth Against the Enemy

The young militants of the Communist "Youth Battalions" very quickly organized an armed Resistance, particularly against uniformed members of the Wehrmacht. In response, the Occupier attempted to prove that "terrorism" had been eradicated, by mounting a series of show trials. These began in March 1942, with one trial being held in the Chamber of Deputies, where seven defendants received seven death sentences. Then, on April 7, came the trial at the Maison de Chimie, which was filmed. Beneath the swastika sat the presiding judge, an ardent Nazi named Gottloeb, who heard arguments from lawyers—mostly Alsatians—chosen mainly for their ability to plead in German. Twenty-seven different French defendants stood before this German military tribunal, all arrested by the French police, turned over to the Occupier, and charged with thirty-four assassinations and acts of sabotage. On arrest, their hands had been manacled behind their backs, where they remained until the defendants testified before the court. Yves Kerman was probably their commander. The Collaborationist press inveighed against "thugs who kill for pay."

1. *German-speaking lawyers in Paris at a German military court trying twenty-seven members of the Resistance, April 1942.*

2, 3. *The convicted prisoners being led away after their trial in a German military court.*

4. *Fifteen-year-old André Kirschen, one of the accused, during his interrogation. The revolver he holds was evidence at the trial against him and his associates.*

5. *Karl Schönhaar, one of the accused.*

6. *Simone Schloss.*

Martyrs to the Cause

One lone accused escaped the charges brought against him. For all the others, the weight of the evidence proved too overwhelming. Pierre Tourette declared: "I regret nothing." Meanwhile, Karl Schönhaar, son of a German Communist deputy assassinated by the Nazis in 1934, lashed out in German at his judges: "Like my father, I shall die for France and for Germany." Twenty-six death sentences had been sought, but since André Kirschen (seen in plate 4 with a 6.35 revolver in his hand) was not yet sixteen and thus subject only to imprisonment, twenty-five would be pronounced. Two women received official pardons. Marie-Thérèse Lefèvre had already been incarcerated at Mauthausen, while Simone Schloss (plate 6) went to the guillotine several weeks later, on July 2, 1942. That left twenty-three to face a firing squad on April 17 at Mont-Valérien. A bit later the Nazis avenged the loss of André Kirschen by arresting his father and brother and executing them as hostages.

4

5

6

Death to the Jews

During the Occupation most Parisian newspapers were noisily anti-Semitic, reflecting either real prejudice or state policy. The most infamous of these rags was *Au Pilori*, "the weekly of the fight against Jewish Masonry." A brief quotation from the March 14, 1941, issue gives a sense of what it was like: "Death to the Jew! Aye, we say again! Death! D.E.A.T.H. TO THE JEW! There! The Jew is no man, but a foul-smelling beast. We pick off fleas. We fight epidemics.... We defend ourselves against disease and death—why not against the Jews?" In April 1944 many of the *Au Pilori* editors, led by Maurice-Ivan Sicard and Henry Coston, took part in the preparation of a 150-page booklet reproducing "500 documents." The title, *I Hate You*, had been taken, out of context, from a statement made by France's pre-war Jewish, Socialist Premier, Léon Blum, who, driven beyond endurance, had turned on the right-wing deputies trying to shout him down. The readers of this special issue could learn about "the Jewing of France,"

which, according to *I Hate You*, began with "the English agent Marat" (*sic*) and continued with the "Jewish invasion" of the movies, the theater, popular music, and mainstream professions (it was well known that "quack doctoring" had been brought to France by the Jews). Also cited was the attempted corruption of young people and the army, as well as, needless to say, the "Jewish plot against peace" and "terrorism, the Jewish weapon."

1, 2. *Anti-Semitic newspapers (CJDC).*

3. *The yellow star, 1942.*

4. *The war-wounded and bemedaled Victor Fajnzylber was exempt from having to wear the yellow star, but not from deportation to a death camp. His six-year-old granddaughter enjoyed no exemption and thus wore the stigmatizing star.*

5. *A café closed to Jews, July 1940.*

6. *A telephone booth off limits to Jews.*

3

4

5

6

A Time of Shame

In 1942 the Occupier decided to treat the Jews as outcasts. The ninth "Decree" of the Military Governor of France, dated July 8, 1942, expressly forbade them admission to restaurants, cafés, theaters, movie houses, concert halls, markets, fairs, swimming pools, sports grounds, racecourses, museums, libraries, and public telephones. They were allowed to do their shopping only between 3 and 4 PM. A few weeks earlier an ordinance dated May 29, 1942, and made effective on June 7 required that all Jews over the age of six in the Occupied Zone wear the yellow Star of David, the symbolic force of which was to designate them *Untermenschen*, subhumans. This "six-pointed device" bearing "the word 'Jew' in black letters" was to be worn "conspicuously on the left breast, firmly sewn to the garment." Anti-Semites, particularly in Collaborationist circles, were jubilant. However, certain Gentiles expressed their support for the Jews by voluntarily donning yellow stars of their own; they were arrested and sometimes even deported.

1. *On the Rue de Rivoli.*

2. *Poster at the entrance to the Hôtel Drouot, July 29, 1941: "Jews are forbidden to enter the auction rooms."*

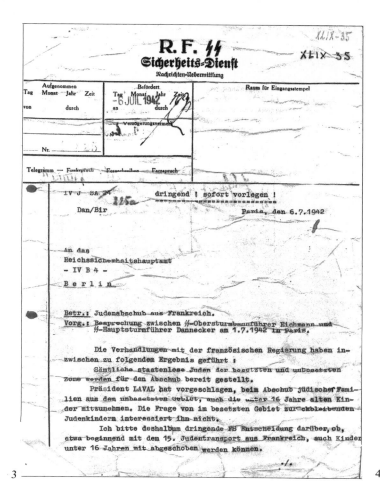

France and the Final Solution

In January 1942, in the Berlin suburb of Wannsee, Nazi leaders decided to launch the "Final Solution," meaning the systematic extermination of all Jews in Occupied Europe. Subsequent to negotiations in June and July 1942 between members of Eichmann's staff and René Bousquet, Secretary-General of Police, the Occupier arranged that roundups of Jews, who by definition were now stateless persons, should be undertaken by the French authorities. Operation *Vent printanier* ("Spring Wind") began to unfold in Paris on July 16–17, 1942, with the result that 900 squads of French police would arrest 3,031 men, 5,802 women, and 3,031 children in the so-called "Vel'd'Hiv' roundup," which involved the detention of whole families, in conditions of unbearable hardship, in the Vélodrome d'Hiver in central Paris. In the Unoccupied Zone, on August 26–28, police emptied the camps where all foreign Jews had been interned since October 4, 1940, and made systematic arrests in "stateless Jewish circles" before loading their victims on trains to Pithiviers, Beaune-la-Rolande, or, most often, Drancy. Laval had even gone beyond the demands of his German masters by turning over to them all children more than two years of age.

3. *Danneker's telegram to Berlin: "President Laval has proposed that when Jewish families are evacuated from the Unoccupied Zone, children under sixteen should accompany them."*

4. *A street search.*

From Drancy to Auschwitz

The first convoy of Jewish deportees rolled out, in third-class carriages, on March 27, 1942, with most of the 743 prominent members of the French Jewish community who had been arrested in Paris on the night of December 11–12, 1941. With four exceptions, all the other convoys of "racial deportees," their cattle cars packed with men and women traveling, in conditions of indescribable horror, towards death of one kind or another. Such was the fate of the class of schoolgirls assembled by the Union Générale des Israélites de France ("General Union of French Jews") who were deported with their teachers in the convoy of July 31, 1944. Upon their arrival at Auschwitz railway station, they were submitted to a "selection" process that divided them into two groups, one of which, made up of children, the elderly, and the weak, went straight to the gas chamber. In all, at least 75,721 Jews disappeared from France, and precise statistics exist for some 70,000 of them (including 10,000 children). Thus, it is known that 23,000 were French and 47,000 foreigners, while 29,000 were "selected" for forced labor, of whom 2,500—3 percent of those shipped out of Drancy—returned after the war.

1. *After three roundups in the Occupied Zone, on May 14, August 30, and December, 12, 1941, the first convoys for the extermination camps left France on March 27, 1942.*

2. *Schoolgirls from the Saint-Mandé Center of the UGIF (see text), deported with their teacher in the convoy of July 31, 1944.*

Early in the winter of 1942, the *Pariser Zeitung*, "Paris' great newspaper," published an illustrated story on the Drancy camp, concluding that the Jews imprisoned there were so comfortable that they had no grounds for complaint. In reality, Drancy was a wretched antechamber to the extermination depots, consisting of a series of four-story structures in the middle of the town, each forming a right-angled "U" around a courtyard. Through its unfinished living quarters there passed, between August 20, 1941, and August 17, 1944, more than 70,000 rounded-up or arrested Jews. These men and—after July 1942—women, not to mention children, some of whom had been torn from their families and shipped alone, were vouchsafed two-tier wooden bunks with skimpy mattresses, one faucet for each room containing about sixty people, and toilets across the courtyard in a separate building. Here the inmates suffered cold and hunger, all the while devoured by fleas and lice. After July 1943 the camp was taken over by the SS. Four convoys left it for extermination camps before July 1942, 40 from July 1942 to July 1943, and 21 from July 1943 to August 1944.

3, 4. *Drancy.*

5. *A page from a Drancy "identity book," showing a receipt issued to Mme Esther Tenenbaum, of Paris, for 5,150 in cash and assorted jewelry.*

6. *Graffiti on a wall at Drancy.*

7. *Jews being deported in 1941.*

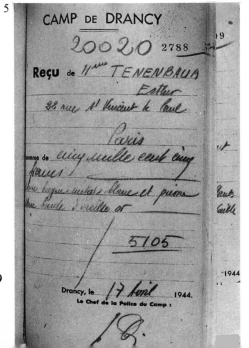

6

7

180

Liberation

Paris Must Not Fall into the Hands of the Enemy

When the Americans broke out at Avranches on July 31—a month after the funeral of Philippe Henriot, the Collaborationist propaganda czar assassinated by the Resistance—Germany lost a crucial battle on the Normandy Front. Parisians enjoyed an unusual parade of military equipment of all kinds, but the Reich had by no means lost the war, and German troops were withdrawing rather than retreating. Paris, an indispensable center of communications, was also regarded by the Wehrmacht brass as an important strategic point. For reasons no less political than military, Hitler had couched his orders in very precise terms: "Paris must not fall to the enemy—or the enemy must find it reduced to rubble." The new Commandant of *Gross-Paris*, General Dietrich von Choltitz, owed this as-

signment to his having not been implicated in the July 20 assassination plot, from which Hitler had miraculously escaped unharmed. Too, he was the commander who had so brutally reduced Sebastopol. The forces at his disposal were not negligible: 17,000 men and a hundred Tiger and Panther tanks.

1. *Funeral of assassinated Philippe Henriot at Notre-Dame, July 1, 1944.*

2. *The Hôtel Majestic with its fortifications, in a photo taken after the Paris Uprising in August 1944.*

3. *At the Rond-Point des Champs-Élysées, trucks camouflaged with foliage returning from the Normandy Front in 1944.*

4. *"To the Normandy Front."*

5. *Returning from the Normandy Front in 1944.*

182

3

Bod.H.-Bekleidungs-Dienststelle
Paris
Vanves   Rue Larmeroux 7

ZUR NORMANDIE FRONT

4

5

A City in Disarray

Since early August 1944 the daily life of the average Parisian had become increasingly complicated and irksome, with no power during the day, with only a half-hour of gas at meal times, with fewer and fewer subways and almost no passenger trains. On August 10 almost all the railroad workers, following an appeal by the National Front, walked out on a patriotic strike. In the background of all this, meanwhile, the Paris Uprising was coming to a boil under the auspices of the Military Commission of the National Resistance Council, founded in May 1943 by Jean Moulin. It met in Paris, with Georges Bidault (general delegate of the Provisional Government of the French Republic and minister-delegate for the Occupied Territories, and, after the war, several times Premier of France) in the chair, and included Alexandre Parodi, a high commissioner of the exiled French government, Jacques Chaban-Delmas, a senior treasury official in exile and national military representative reporting to General Koenig, and the Paris Liberation Committee, which comprised all shades of opinion within the Resistance. In plate 5, taken immediately after the Liberation, may be seen Daniel Mayer, Socialist representative on the Committee, Marie-Hélène Lefaucheux of the Organisation Civile et Militaire, Georges Marrane of the Front National, Léo Hamon of the Mouvement de Libération Nationale, and Rol-Tanguy, a former member of the International Brigades in the Spanish Civil War and now head of the FFI (Forces Françaises de l'Intérieur, the underground group sponsored by the Communist Party) for Region "P," the Île-de-France.

1. *The Gare Saint-Lazare, 1944. With the trains out of service trucks take Parisians to the suburbs.*

2. *Gare Saint-Lazare, 1944.*

3. *Daniel Mayer.*

4. *Jacques Chaban-Delmas.*

5. *The Paris Liberation Committee, August 1944: (left to right) Maynial, Obadia, Rigal, Léo Hamon, Colonel Rol-Tanguy, Carrel, Demare, Tollet, Mme Lefaucheux, Marrane.*

3

4

5

185

Aux Armes, Citoyens!

On Saturday August 19, Alexandre Parodi, General Representative of the Provisional Government of the French Republic, acting on the resolution taken by the National Resistance Committee, decreed the mobilization of all male Parisians between 18 and 55 and summoned them to arms. It was the beginning of an eventful week. Initially, the Uprising took the Germans by surprise, and the insurgents occupied a number of public structures including town halls and—most important—police headquarters, where members of the three Resistance groups within the police force dug themselves in. German trucks were stopped and weapons seized by men in tricolore armbands overprinted with the Cross of Lorraine (Gaullist), or with the initials FFI (Communist) or FTP (independent). But even Rol-Tanguy, with his 20,000 effectives, could not hope to arm every one of them.

186

4

5

1. *During the attack on the town hall of Neuilly on August 19, 1944, the sculptor Maillard was killed on his own doorstep by a burst of machine-gun fire from an SS vehicle.*

2. *A casualty of the street fighting.*

3. *Police headquarters, August 19, 1944.*

4. *Irregulars on the Pont-Neuf.*

5. *Insurgent Parisian marksmen behind a barricaded window.*

To the Barricades

If its members disagreed on practical modalities, the Parisian Resistance—virtually to a man and a woman—accepted as a common objective the declaration made by Charles de Gaulle on April 18, 1942: "The National Liberation cannot be separated from national insurrection." To their eyes, it was a matter of principle that Frenchmen and Parisians must not stand by and simply wait to be delivered from the enemy. Those active in the Resistance were perfectly aware of the risks involved, but they assumed that the element of surprise would work in their favor and that urban guerrilla warfare would prove effective. Once the truce had been broken in August 1944, the Gavroche Paris of Victor Hugo's *Les Misérables* rose again in certain quarters, with some 400 street barricades built from civil-defense sandbags and wood as well as sandstone paving blocks. Thanks to the Spanish Civil War, the insurgents also knew how to mix Molotov cocktails from petrol, sulfuric acid, and potassium permanganate.

1. *A street barricade.*
2. *Mixing Molotov cocktails.*

Union des Femmes Françaises
(Adhérentes au Front National)

Aux Femmes de Paris

Malgré les bruits d'armistice les Allemands continuent de tuer les Français. Ne laissons pas désarmer les nôtres, n'aidons pas les assassins SS. La lutte continue.

Dans Paris toujours occupé, les F.F.I. et les Milices Patriotiques se battent avec courage. Des femmes sont à leur côté, les armes à la main, suivons leur exemple.

· Par tous les moyens, aidons ces braves : ils ont faim, portons-leur du pain. Sortons pour eux nos réserves. Ils ont soif, portons-leur à boire. Jour et nuit ravitaillons-les. Recueillons et soignons les blessés. Organisons-nous en groupes de la Milice Patriotique.

Grâce aux F.F.I. et aux Milices Patriotiques soutenues par la population tout entière,

Paris, bientôt, sera libre !

L'UNION DES FEMMES FRANÇAISES.

A Brief Lull before the Storm

Some of the insurgents feared that the confrontation with the Occupier might turn into a territorial struggle—in which the Resistance would be fatally disadvantaged—or lead to a revolution. Thus, they quickly accepted the terms of the truce negotiated by the Swedish Consul General, Raoul Nordling, who thereby obtained the release of numerous political detainees. Moreover, the truce between the Germans and the FFI was well received by the population at large. But within the Resistance it came in for severe criticism from those—Communists and others—who thought that the reprieve merely enabled the adversary to summon reinforcements and allow free passage for a Wehrmacht now beating a rapid retreat. Finally, the truce was little honored by either side, since the SS units refused to let it work.

3. *Tract by the Union of French Women.*

4. *The truce of August 20, 1944.*

3

Death to Huns and Traitors!

On Tuesday, August 22, the Resistance leaders decided, after stormy discussion, to break the truce and resume fighting. Barricades went up in many neighborhoods. The uprising was directed by Rol-Tanguy in his capacity as FFI commander, from his underground headquarters 118 steps below the Lion of Belfort statue on the Place Denfert-Rochereau. However, the situation remained confused, since the Germans stubbornly clung to a dozen strongholds from which they could not be driven with the weapons available to the insurgents. Increasingly, it became clear that help would be needed from the French and Anglo-American forces outside the city.

1. *Colonel Rol-Tanguy's secret command-post in the catacombs beneath Place Denfert-Rochereau.*

2. *A Communist Party proclamation posted over a portrait of Philippe Henriot, the Collaborationist assassinated on June 28, 1944.*

3. L'Humanité, *August 22, 1944:* "DEATH TO GERMANS AND TRAITORS! *Parisians! Stand up and Fight!*"

4. *Avenue de l'Opéra, August 20, 1944.*

5. *August 22–23, 1944.*

War Comes to the Streets

Unlike Warsaw, Paris was not the scene of a general engagement, and there were neighborhoods where nothing very much happened. Even where fighting did occur, the indifferent and the skeptical were always numerous, to say nothing of those who preferred to battle by telephone, those who joined at the last minute, the curious, and the idlers. Housewives continued to queue throughout a city where flour stocks had declined to a mere week's supply. Between clashes the dead were buried, and the first-aid teams of the National Doctors' Front and the National Health Service stood ready in their whitewashed steel helmets. They had their hands full when tracer shells set fire to the FFI-held Grand Palais, setting the building ablaze and trapping its garrison.

1. *A child wounded on the Rue de Rivoli.*

2. *A first-aid team near Saint-Sévérin.*

3. *Caskets of FFI members killed in the fighting.*

4. *The Grand Palais gutted by fire.*

5. *The Porte Saint-Denis, August 1944.*

4

5

Leclerc Liberates Paris

Thanks to Rolland Gallois, who made his way through the German lines, General Eisenhower gained a very exact picture of the situation developing in Paris. The Supreme Allied Commander had initially intended, mostly for reasons of logistics, to advance beyond Paris without a siege, but, after weighing his responsibilities, he decided, rightly enough, that Paris must be liberated—and by French troops. He ordered the 2nd Armored Division, with 15,000 men and 200 tanks, which was near Argentan after taking part in the Normandy campaign, to advance on the capital. The mighty vehicles covered 150 miles in 40 hours, with Leclerc's men advancing along two lines: Jouy-en-Josas–Porte de Saint-Cloud, and Longjumeau–Bourg-la-Reine. In the afternoon of Thursday 24 an aircraft flying at rooftop height dropped a weighted message: "Hold fast; we're coming—Leclerc." A few hours later, on a fine summer evening, several jeeps and the tanks "Romilly," "Champaubert," and "Montmirail," of the 1st Chad Infantry Regiment, nosed through the Porte d'Orléans and made their way to the Place de l'Hôtel de Ville. Early the next morning they were followed by other units of the 2nd Armored.

1. *General Leclerc's troops entering Paris, August 25. 1944.*

Taking Out the Last of the German Strongholds

On Friday, August 25, Leclerc's forces put into effect the fire-power needed to take out the remaining German strongholds. Often the Resistance and the Free French joined forces in sharp encounters with the Germans—for example, at the Luxembourg Garden and the Senate, where SS units had dug in, and at the barracks on the Place de la République, which held out for six hours, at the Ministry of Foreign Affairs, and at the Naval Ministry in the Place de la Concorde. The 2nd Armored lost 130 killed and 329 wounded, while about 1,000 insurgents and almost 2,000 "civilians" perished. Some 2,000 Germans would never again cross the Rhine.

2

2. *A tank named "Auersthedt" in front of Notre-Dame.*

3. *Attack on the Senate Building, Boulevard Saint-Michel, August 25, 1944.*

3

Surrender at Last

On Friday, August 25, the Germans began to give themselves up wholesale. They were on the run, their morale had evaporated, and they hoped to be taken prisoner by Anglo-American, or at worst by French regular, units rather than by the Resistance, at whose hands they feared reprisals. They came out, hands held high, to a general chorus of boos and insults, and some came in for rough handling. Dietrich von Choltitz decided not to carry out his Führer's orders, to leave Paris in ruins, since, like many high-ranking German officers, he had, since July 20, lost considerable faith in the Reich's ultimate victory. The Hôtel Meurice gave way after an attack lasting two hours, and the Commandant of *Gross-Paris* was led off to police headquarters, where, at 3:30 PM, he signed an "instrument of surrender" in the presence of General Leclerc (Rol-Tanguy got to affix his signature a little later). Taken to 2nd Armored HQ, he drew up orders for his garrison to cease fire, and for the most part they were obeyed.

3

1

2

4

1. *German prisoners outside the Luxembourg Garden railings.*

2. *The capture of the École Militaire, August 25, 1944, with a jeep from the 4th Squadron, 12th Cuirassier Regiment, 2nd Armored Division, on its way to Dupleix with a German officer and NCO seeking to negotiate a surrender.*

3. *After the surrender of the Senate (the Luxembourg), German wounded being evacuated.*

4. *Prisoners of the FFI.*

5. *German prisoners on the Rue de Rivoli, August 25, 1944.*

Liberation and Joy

By Saturday, August 26, the city of Paris, if not its suburbs, had been effectively liberated, and Leclerc's men paused to catch their breath in jeeps, trucks, and tanks demurely parked in the great squares. Parisians—not only those who had taken part in the Uprising but also the onetime bystanders and skeptics—made haste to greet their much-traveled liberators. It would be a day of apotheosis, beginning with the stately progress of General Charles de Gaulle, President of the French Republic's provisional government, from the Arc de Triomphe all the way to Notre-Dame. First, he reviewed the 2nd Armored and then proceeded down the Champs-Élysées, leading a retinue of men and women who had survived the four-year Occupation to play an important role in France's internal Resistance or in the forces of Free France abroad. Later de Gaulle would write, in his *War Memoirs*: "Ah, it was a sea of people, a crowd filling the whole of the roadway. . . ." It was indeed—a human sea, united in the joy of the moment, and united in the conviction that a chapter had been closed once and for all. Meanwhile, the American vanguard was moving through the eastern suburbs, ready to intervene should the need arise.

1. *The arrival of the Americans, August 25, 1944.*
2. *Place de l'Hôtel-de-Ville, August 26, 1944.*
3. *Place de la Concorde, August 26, 1944.*

The Last Shots

The victory parade was marred by random bursts of gunfire, whose perpetrators could seldom be caught red-handed. The FFI and the men of the 2nd Armored were both targeted by individual sharpshooters apparently firing from rooftops. Sporadic shots rang out as the parade reached the Avenue George-V and increased when it entered the Place de la Concorde. One report seemingly set off by accident triggered a veritable fusillade before and within Notre-Dame, where the resulting chaos left dozens of people wounded. It is now known that some members of the Collaborationist Militia had decided to fire parting shots in the capital before fleeing eastward. One of those killed in this desperate violence was the assassin of Georges Mandel, the respected Jewish politician and member of France's prewar government whom the Militia had murdered earlier in 1944. Still, the war went on, and in the night of August 26–27 shells fired by German units counter-attacking from Le Bourget killed about fifty Parisians.

1. *Place de la Concorde, August 26, 1944.*

2, 3. *The fusillade in the Place de la Concorde, August 26, 1944.*

1

2

3

De Gaulle Meets His Destiny

The two men who came face to face outside Notre-Dame were, in the eyes of many of the city's inhabitants, the living symbols of liberated Paris. Captain Philippe de Hautecloque, wounded and captured during the campaign of 1940, escaped and immediately joined the Free French, taking the pseudonym of Leclerc in order to protect his family. He was present when French Equatorial Africa joined the Free French, captured Koufra, and there issued an Order of the Day to the Chad Infantry Regiment telling them that they would go forward until the tricolore floated once more over Strasbourg Cathedral. For the nonce, the Commander of the 2nd Armored was content to see it flying from the towers of Notre-Dame. De Gaulle, "the man of June 18," had served his time in the political desert and was now head of France's Provisional Government. Six weeks earlier, he had forcibly persuaded President Roosevelt that France must be governed and administered by Frenchmen alone. Now the proud Lorrainer was back in Paris, by way of Brittany where he had been happily mobbed by his admirers. In his eagerness to become a Parisian again, de Gaulle went straight from Leclerc's headquarters to his old office on the Rue Saint-Dominique, which he had occupied in June 1940 as Under-Secretary of State for War. He came out, making a swing through police headquarters, to celebrate the people of Paris at the Hôtel de Ville. By their popular acclaim, they endowed the man who had stood alone on June 18, 1940, with the stature of a Head of State. It was his self-imposed mission to make that State once again whole and entire.

1

2

1. *General de Gaulle with General Leclerc outside Notre-Dame.*

2. *Leclerc outside Notre-Dame.*

Revenge and Reprisal

The memory of the dead, of all the dead, intruded even on the rejoicing of those days. There were the men and women killed by a stray bullet or cut down in the fighting, as well as the last victims of Nazi vindictiveness, members of the Resistance murdered at Vincennes, at the Fort de Romainville, or at the Luxembourg, and the thirty-five young people—average age seventeen—summarily executed by a French Gestapo man near the waterfall in the Bois de Boulogne. Before the fighting stopped, the cleansing had begun. Its first targets were members of the Militia, Collaborationists, and women vulgarly referred to as "horizontal Collaborationists." Naked or half-naked, their heads shaven, these unfortunates often found themselves paraded before jeering crowds moved as much by voyeurism as by political righteousness. But the average Parisian slept peacefully through the night of Saturday, August 26, confident that all his tomorrows would be coming up roses.

1. *A scene in the courtyard of the Prefecture of Police.*

2. *A tank in which three French soldiers died during the Paris Uprising.*

1

2

Evening, August 26, 1944.

INDEX OF NAMES

ACKNOWLEDGEMENTS AND PHOTO CREDITS

The publisher would like to express his profound gratitude to those whose assistance and valued cooperation made this book possible.

A.D.N. ZENTRALBILD (Berlin RDA) *(59, 61, 62, 66, 69, 72, 76, 97, 98, 99, 133, 134).*

L'A.F.P. *(185).*

The Cabinet des estampes et de la photographie and the photographic service of the BIBLIOTHÈQUE NATIONALE *(59, 82, 84, 85, 100, 102, 103, 105, 132, 133, 135, 137, 144, 150, 151, 152, 156, 158, 166, 170, 175, 176, Seeberger 130).*

BILDARCHIV (Berlin RFA) *(63, 66, 67, 68, 70, 88, 172, 173, 180).*

Mme Gilberte BRASSAÏ *(121, 168).*

LA CAISSE NATIONALE DES MONUMENTS HISTORIQUES ET DES SITES *(Seeberger 123, 126, 127, 149, 154, 159).*

M. Vidar Jacobsen, of the CENTRE JUIF DE DOCUMENTATION CONTEMPORAINE *(174, 175, 177, 178, 179).*

Mme Christine Petiteau of the CINÉMATHÈQUE FRANÇAISE *(106, 107, 109).*

Mme Hélène Kouza and Mme Geneviève de Tarragon of the AGENCE EDIMEDIA *(60, 89, 100, 112, 140, 155, 159, 164, 165, 166, 189, 190.* Imperial War Museum - Edimedia *95, 104, 192).*

Mme GEMÄHLING

R. GENDRE *(60, 88, 98, 117, 124, 169, 170, 186, 191, 193).*

M. Jacques Kanapa and the ARCHIVES PHOTOGRAPHIQUES OF L'HUMANITÉ *(82, 90, 96, 97, 100, 120, 166, 177, 182, 185, 190).*

L'ILLUSTRATION *(59, 90, 126, 132).*

PIERRE JAHAN *(151, 183).*

KEYSTONE *(69, 185).*

Mme SERGE LIDO *(111, 112, 116, 131).*

MAGNUM *(168).*

Mme Thérèse Blondet, head of the photoservice of the MUSÉE DES DEUX GUERRES MONDIALES (B.D.I.C.) *(61, 126, 154, 164, 170, 171, 187, 194).*

Mme Claire PAULHAN *(169).*

M. et Mme Edouard PIGNON *(120 Willy Ronis).*

RAPHO (Robert Doisneau : *160, 163, 167, 191, 192).*

ROGER-VIOLLET *(92, 93, 95, 103, 118, 124, 125, 144, 168, 169).*

WILLY RONIS *(120).*

ROGER SCHALL *(19, 48, 62, 63, 64, 65, 70, 71, 73, 74, 75, 76, 77, 78, 79, 80, 81, 83, 84, 86, 91, 111, 131, 136, 137, 138, 139, 140, 141, 142, 143, 145, 146, 148, 156, 157, 158, 161, 162, 170, 175, 183, 184, 186, 196, 200, 202).*

ALBERT SEEBERGER *(54, 109, 110, 114, 115, 117, 118, 119, 128, 129, 139, 147, 148, 184, 187, 188, 189, 193, 195, 197, 198, 199, 204).*

Mme Chalufour of ÉDITIONS TALLANDIER *(58, 65, 74, 94, 107).*

M. Pierre ZUCCA *(8, 28, 82, 92, 93, 101, 102, 104, 107, 110, 113, 122, 127, 176, 182).*

The publisher would also like to acknowledge the help of Mme Annette Arnstam-Doisneau, M. Guy Desgranges of the librairie ARMAND COLIN, M. Michel Kempf, photographer and M. Lucien Treillard.